Mastering Stocks and Bonds

Mastering Stocks and Bonds

Understanding How Asset Cross-Over Strategies Will Improve Your Portfolio's Performance

Ben Emons

palgrave
macmillan

MASTERING STOCKS AND BONDS

Copyright © Ben Emons, 2015.

All rights reserved.

First published in 2015 by
PALGRAVE MACMILLAN®
in the United States—a division of St. Martin's Press LLC,
175 Fifth Avenue, New York, NY 10010.

Where this book is distributed in the UK, Europe and the rest of the world,
this is by Palgrave Macmillan, a division of Macmillan Publishers Limited,
registered in England, company number 785998, of Houndmills,
Basingstoke, Hampshire RG21 6XS.

Palgrave Macmillan is the global academic imprint of the above companies
and has companies and representatives throughout the world.

Palgrave® and Macmillan® are registered trademarks in the United States,
the United Kingdom, Europe and other countries.

ISBN: 978–1–137–47624–1

Library of Congress Cataloging-in-Publication Data

Emons, Ben.
    Mastering stocks and bonds : understanding how asset cross-over
    strategies will improve your portfolio's performance / Ben Emons.
        pages cm
    Includes bibliographical references and index.
    ISBN 978–1–137–47624–1—
    ISBN 1–137–47624–9
        1. Investments. 2. Portfolio management. I. Title.

HG4521.E5243 2015
332.63'2—dc23   2015009369

A catalogue record of the book is available from the British Library.

Design by Newgen Knowledge Works (P) Ltd., Chennai, India.

First edition: September 2015

10 9 8 7 6 5 4 3 2 1

Printed in the United States of America.

Contents

Figures and Tables

Figures

Tables

1
The Cross-over

I magine you had a choice between only two investments: stocks and bonds. Which would you choose? Investors in bonds are conservative, seek stable income and have a longer-term investment horizon. Investors who purchase stocks are "aggressive" and want high returns in a shorter period of time. The distinction between stocks and bonds has been in place since the 1920s, when investing became popular. The distinction has been quantified by a correlation that has been mostly negative between the price of bonds and the price of stocks. Investors who seek diversification would therefore have a portfolio of bonds and stocks, for example, weighted by 40 percent in bonds and 60 percent in stocks. The question of which of the two investments would be the top choice is answered by the weights of each in the portfolio. The answer should also focus on the cross-over return between the two asset classes. The cross-over return is defined as the return on bonds that is influenced by the return on stocks and vice versa. Investors may not understand how much, in certain periods, the returns of bonds can be closely correlated with stock returns. The future returns of bonds and stocks may be influenced significantly by the cross-over return. When monetary policymakers use stocks and bonds to stage a sustainable economic recovery, the correlation between stocks and bonds is an important factor to consider in asset allocation decisions. Often investors look at valuation to determine whether the correlation will change. Perhaps more specifically, the way Benjamin Graham in his book *Security Analysis* (1934) described intrinsic value as "in general terms, it is understood to that intrinsic value is justified by the facts (e.g., the assets, earnings, dividends, definite prospects as distinct, let us say, from market quotations established by artificial manipulation or distorted by psychological excesses). But, it is a great mistake to imagine that intrinsic value is as definite and as determinable as is the market price" (Graham, 1934, p. 68).

Although Benjamin Graham's point is greatly relevant, the intrinsic value of individual stocks and bonds is where a cross-over return opportunity resides. In today's marketplace, it is critical to understand how intrinsic value has been influenced by factors such as global capital flows and monetary policy. There are several aspects to the "cross-over perspective" of investing. A person who invests in bonds may have a different mind-set than a person who invests in stocks. Neither may be aware of how the other may think when it comes to asset allocation. Several studies on investor behavior by the Federal Reserve (Bernanke, 2003), suggest that bond and stock investors have "active" and "passive" asset allocation tendencies. Active management is best described as "bargain hunting." Every day there are "good deals" or "bad choices" in financial markets. Active management is a method to identify securities that are "good deals" and those that would be a "bad choice." In active investment management there are methods used such as fundamental analysis, technical analysis, and macroeconomic analysis. These methods are typically combined in an investment strategy to spot trends in the economy and market place. Passive investment management on the other hand does not distinguish individual securities, neither to predict their price movements nor to actively time markets. A passive manager invests in the broad market, like the S&P 500 Index. A passive manager has a similar motivation as an active manager: to make a profit. The difference between passive and active managers is the former is willing to accept the average market index return. The active manager on the other hand does not accept earning just the benchmark index return. These managers actively seek opportunities outside the index universe to generate excess return. Active managers are called "alpha" investors, whereby alpha is defined as the return in excess of the index return. In principle, there should be no difference between an equity and a bond investor in the application of active or passive strategies. There are, however, different ways of investing passively or actively in bonds as compared to stocks. An active fixed-income approach to a stock portfolio is an example of a "cross-over strategy." Thinking of such a strategy, one has to identify the difference characteristics of bond and stock investors.

A bond investor applies a different set of methods to identify value than an equity investor does. For example, investing in bonds requires an understanding of yield curve, duration, and convexity. There are differences between bonds in terms of risk premiums ("spreads"), yields, and liquidity. Bonds are about the reinvestment principle of interest and principal, rolling down the yield curve, and earning "carry" over holding a portfolio in cash. There are also fixed-income managers who specialize in arbitrage and relative value. These fixed-income concepts are often not applicable to equity investing. A stock investor looks at earnings of a company and compares the stock within a specific sector and to the broader market. An equity investor can, however, apply fixed-income techniques to asset allocation. At the same time, bond investors can incorporate equity investing principles in their investment strategy. For example, credit analysis, albeit traditionally applied in selecting investment-grade and high-yield bonds, is rarely applied when assessing government bonds, agency bonds, and municipal bonds. Equity investing, in contrast, uses methods for comparing return on equity (ROE) or invested capital to the cost of capital. A return on equity calculation applied to a bond is a measure for determining how much institutional demand there is for fixed-income securities. For banks, for example, holding government bonds became a profitable business because of the Federal Reserve's quantitative easing policies since November 2008. Government bonds became therefore an earnings generator. This is a reason why return on equity could be applied in fixed-income analysis. The demand by institutions may therefore materially impact future returns on fixed income. A stock is traditionally valued based upon its price-to-earnings (PE) ratio, but the calculation can be applied to bonds as well. Similarly, the yield curve on which bonds are evaluated can be applied to equities by constructing an equity yield curve. A stock value can be calculated from discounting dividends or by using a forward price-earnings ratio. Stocks, like bonds, have duration. By discounting a stock's present value over its dividend yield, a stock's duration is the weighted average time dividends are paid. Equity duration, however, is not static number because stocks are not issued with a final maturity. Based on general dividend payout policy, equity duration is measured as the reciprocal of the dividend yield. On average, equity duration can be as long as 30 years, but may fluctuate significantly if dividend payout ratios change.

People who invest in stocks and bonds have a different styles and different investment horizons. A cross-over strategy focused on investing in companies at numerous stages of the business life cycle can support a successful mix of stocks and bonds in a portfolio. The strategy is the direct opposite of the buy-and-hold method, in which the investor does not trade between the period when a security is first bought and when it is finally sold. The goal of the cross-over strategy is to get the best returns during shorter periods of time (three months up to a year). A buy-and-hold method focuses on long-term growth. Cross-over investing has been applied in specialized products. There are convertible bonds that are hybrid securities in which bond holders can convert a bond into common stock. A convertible bond also involves merger and acquisition arbitrage. That arbitrage is subjected to corporate governance and entails dividend policy and earnings. There are other "debt for equity" securities, such as contingent capital notes issued by financial institutions, subordinated debt, and distressed corporate debt. Investment-grade corporate bonds can trade closer in price terms to subordinated debt when there is financial stress. In other words, when bonds have higher credit risk, they may behave more like equity in times of high price volatility. Historically, there has been a positive correlation between the broader equity market and investment-grade and high-yield fixed-income securities when markets experience upheavals.

Cross-over investing also addresses several other issues, such as market technical factors, supply and demand, and risk premium. Liquidity in bonds and stocks is generally determined in a similar way (as it is for currencies and commodities), and measured by a bid-and-ask price quoted by dealers and market makers. Stocks and bonds are traded electronically, and individual stock futures were introduced in recent years. Dealers' treatment of inventory does not always discriminate between bonds and stocks because they are subject to a similar risk budget set by management. The financing of bonds and stocks in terms of a collateral swap works relatively similarly too. Both bonds and stocks can be borrowed or lent on margin. In terms of flows, bond funds have seen a surge since 2009. This increase has been fueled by uncertainty as to why people would rather save by investing in securities than borrow to start a business. Market commentators view this surge as a result of Federal Reserve policy that attracted risk taking in financial markets. As a result, flows in stock and bonds funds have been in lockstep since 2009. Flows into stock index funds and government bond funds have been at a high record following the 2008 financial crisis. In a modestly recovering economy with inflation but ongoing uncertainty, interest rates and stock prices tend to move closely together. This is likely why people have been diversifying between stocks and bonds. The relationship has strengthened by way of flows into stock and bond funds. Figure 1.1 on page 9 demonstrates the trend. Bond funds in particular have moved more than $1 trillion away from their normal growth trend. Equity funds have remained below the trend since the early 2000s.

The relationship between bonds and stocks can be put into a framework. When interest rates rise in an orderly way, stock prices tend to rise because a rising rate environment contains future inflation and ensures stable economic growth. Stable economic growth and moderate inflation should be positive for companies' future earnings, and

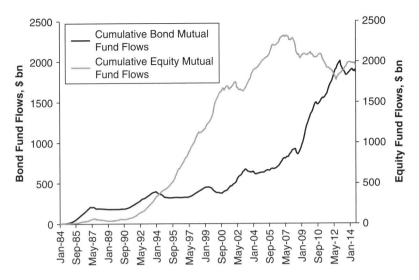

Figure 1.1 Total stock and bond fund flows.
Source: ICI Mutual Fund series (www.ICI.com).

hence supportive for stock prices. Bond prices go down when interest rates rise but if inflation remains moderate, longer term interest rates tend to stabilize. There is also an inverse relationship between stocks and bonds. When interest rates fall (bond prices go up), stimulus is provided to the economy. The value of stock prices goes up because future earnings are discounted at a lower interest rate.

From a cross-over investing perspective, stocks and bonds have several unique features. They provide duration risk, liquidity, and credit quality to a portfolio. It should be emphasized, however, that a bond is *not* the same as a stock and vice versa. Rather the correlation between their returns to the overall market can be highly positive during certain periods. Bonds and stocks therefore both play an important role in asset allocation decisions. The decisions can be made by using a top-down macro view. Decisions to allocate between bonds and stocks also involve bottom-up analysis. One of the most important macro factors is the

Federal Reserve. Since the late 1990s, Fed policy has increasingly focused on the volatility of asset prices.

Valuation: The Fed Model

From a top-down macro view, the "Fed model" is commonly used for equity valuations. Since the late 1990s, the concept of a "put" purchased on the S&P 500 Index by the Federal Reserve has become popular in the media. The "Greenspan put" is one that market observers closely follow. The put gained attention after the 1997 Humprey Hawkins testimony, when former Federal Reserve Chairman Alan Greenspan explained how the Fed looks at stock valuations. The Fed model compares the stock market's earnings yield to the yield on a long-term government bond. The earnings yield is the reciprocal of the S&P 500 Index price-to-earnings ratio. According to the model, the bond and stock market are in equilibrium, and fairly valued, when the one-year forward-looking earnings yield equals the ten-year Treasury yield. The Fed model expresses a relationship between stock- and bondholders in terms of options analogy. A bond can be seen as a put on the future success of the company. Basically, an investor who is buying a bond expects to receive a fixed coupon return and the initial investable amount (typically $1,000) returned at maturity. If the company experiences trouble or default, the bondholder has a claim on the company's assets. A stock is a call on the future success of the company. A stock investor receives a dividend in the form of shares or cash. When the company sees profits turn to losses, an equity holder could eventually get wiped out. In case of a liquidation, equity holders own a put on the firm because equity stakeholders owe principal and interest to the bondholders. The bondholders own a call because in a liquidation, they will be paid before the equity holders. The Fed model has been advanced by calculating the Greenspan put as the difference between the reciprocal of the actual PE Index ratio and the adjusted Index Price/Earnings ratio. The adjusted PE ratio is the long-term real interest rate minus expected earnings growth. Figure 1.2 shows historically the Greenspan put and the Bernanke call.

Back in the 2000s, the Greenspan put premium was close to 3 percent when stock prices were at record highs, but nowadays it is more or less worthless. When Bernanke took over as chairman of the Federal Reserve in 2006, market participants wondered if he would continue the Greenspan put policy. Less than two years after taking office, Bernanke faced the biggest financial crisis in history. In November 2002, he delivered a speech titled "Deflation, Let's Make Sure It Doesn't Happen Here" at the National Economist Club in Washington, DC, in which he outlined several measures for combating deflation risk and a financial crisis by buying unlimited short-maturity government bonds. Bernanke's policy can be viewed as an insurance for bondholders. To calculate the "Bernanke put," the put-call parity may provide an answer. The put-call parity formula is the stock price plus put = call plus value of a zero coupon bond. The assumption is that Greenspan put benefits the stockholders the Bernanke put is beneficial to bondholders. In other words, the Bernanke put is a "call" on bonds. That is because when the Federal Reserve buys US Treasuries, it supports the price of bonds. This has a payoff profile like a call on an underlying asset. There is limited downside, because if interest rates were to rise too fast, the Federal Reserve would buy more Treasury bonds to keep yields low. When plugging the Greenspan put into the put-call parity there are two additional assumptions. The first one is the S&P 500 Index's dividend yields that approximates the return for the stockholder. The other one is the ten-year real interest rate taken from Treasury Inflation Protected Securities. This real interest rate represents the real return for the bondholder.

The Bernanke put fell to zero in 2014 as the Federal Reserve ended its third quantitative easing (QE) program. A few years earlier, it was as high as 1.5 percent, as shown in Figure 1.2. This put-call comparison says that when monetary policy favors one set of stakeholders, investors are enticed to support other stakeholders. Under Greenspan, stockholders were favored by Fed policy. This led to a sharp rise in major equity indices by the late 1990s, but the subsequent crash drove investors into bonds. Following the 2008 financial crisis, Fed policy shifted to support bondholders with quantitative easing. This led to a "taper tantrum crisis" in 2013 when then-Fed chairman Bernanke signaled an end to quantitative easing (QE). As a result, investors have been gradually rotating from bonds into stocks. The

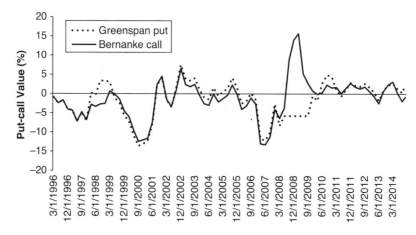

Figure 1.2   The Greenspan put and the Bernanke call.

Source: Federal Reserve Board, Greenspan Put = 1/actual PE ratio – adjusted PE ratio. Bernanke call = Greenspan put – Equity index dividend yield – ten-year real yield from Tips.

*Adjusted PE ratio = ten-year real yield from Treasury Inflation Protected Securities (Tips) – expected earnings growth (Index EPS).

central bank put and call is theoretical, but is significant for financial markets. Because of these central bank put policies, stock and bond markets may at times trade at very different valuations. A subtle change happened in 2013, whereby QE was no longer seen as effective. Political arguments pointed out that QE caused income inequality. At the same time, central banks have kept short-term interest rates near zero because inflation has remained very low. Although short-term interest rates are expected to lift gradually in the future, if the economy were to face a recession, the capacity for central banks to cut interest rates has sharply diminished. The Greenspan put and the Bernanke call can therefore move quickly back in the money because quantitative easing would return to support the economy. Like an option, its value moves "in the money" when the market price of the underlying asset rises above the strike price. This is largely the result of rising volatility. Monetary policy could be viewed that way, whereas the policy action (e.g. quantitative easing) drives up asset prices well above what investors generally expected given the direction of the economy. The Greenspan put and Bernanke call option move "in the money" as asset prices rise above fundamental values. This is a powerful tool that central banks may continue to use to achieve their mandate goals. As a result, bond and stock investors may continue to face a landscape in which monetary policy plays an important role in influencing asset prices. Hence, this is why the theoretical Greenspan put, the Bernanke call, and, perhaps in the future, the Janet Yellen put will remain relevant.

Dividend Discount Model

There are different ideas about how to value equities. Several economists say stocks should be valued as the present value of dividend payments. Nobel Laureate economist Paul Krugman is an advocate of that approach. He said on his Massachusetts Institute of Technology (MIT) website in 2006 that "earnings are not the same as dividends, by a long shot; and what a stock is worth is the present discounted value of the dividends on that stock." Franco Modigliani and Merton Miller posited in their famous 1958 article "The Cost of Capital, Corporation Finance and the Theory of Investment" the "irrelevance" of dividend policy. That is, the underlying expected earnings and cash flow of companies, not their dividend payouts, determine market values. There are models such as the risk premium facto model that show that earnings and interest rates drive the value of the stocks, not the dividend stream. The dividend policy of companies is a choice: they use dividends to repatriate cash to shareholders or choose not to pay dividends in order to reinvest in their business. Some companies borrow to sustain or increase dividends as part of a decision to include more debt in their capital structures, or finance share buybacks. With debt financing on the rise, investors should demand more current yield from their stockholdings because future price appreciation may be at higher risk. To think in terms of "yield," equity investors look at an earnings yield or dividend yield. Bond investors earn a fixed or floating coupon that is discounted over a yield to maturity over the life of the bond investment.

In recent years, in a growing number of instances, dividend yields on stocks have been exceeding the yields on corporate bonds issued by the same company. Although dividend-paying stocks are not riskless, an investor may fare equally well with a portfolio of steady dividend-paying stocks versus a portfolio of high-rated corporate bonds. Investors can find opportunities when they dissect the market and drill down to industry-level comparisons. This has become a further pressing issue in asset allocation strategies because low bond and dividend yields created a "conundrum." Of the 321 companies reporting in the S&P 500 that have pension plans, the median expected in 2013 a rate of return on their plan assets of about 7.7 percent. Their market cap weighted return was 7.5 percent, and the average corporate debt-to-cash holding stood at 42 percent, but their dividend yield was close to 3 percent. The average corporate bonds yielding also near 3.5 percent. In their projections, pension plans may assume equities will deliver high (expected) returns in the future. With record low yields and historically tight corporate bond risk premiums, attention has been drawn to the total return of the equities. This return would include both the current yield, the growth of the dividends, and the price appreciation of the underlying stocks. Dividend growth is unknown. There can be various methods for arriving at an estimate from sample data:

- Five-year historic median growth rate per year is 8 percent.
- The Bloomberg median dividend projected three-year growth is 10 percent.
- The median consensus estimates of dividend for the next three years is 9 percent.
- The median consensus estimates for earnings-per-share (EPS) growth for the next three years is 9 percent.
- The median consensus estimate for Sales growth for the next three years is 5.6 percent.
- The implied improvement in profit margin is +1.5 percent over the next three years.
- The median PE ratio is 18x (earnings yield of 5.5%).

Financial theory developed a model that became famous among academics, but perhaps less so among investors. This is the "dividend discount model" (DDM), which was

originated by Myron Gordon in 1959. This model values
the price of a stock by using predicted dividends and discounting them back to present value. If the value obtained
from the DDM is higher than what the shares are currently
trading at, the stock is undervalued. This model calculates
a stock's value such that the sum of the dividend yield and
the growth rate equals the investor's required total return.
Although the model is derived only from dividends, the
investor will in practice realize the returns from growth
as capital gains. By using different dividend growth estimates and assuming a level of interest rates, Figure 1.3
models two different paths of dividend income streams.
Importantly, there are different assumptions that demonstrate how "sensitive" the value of a stock can be to
interest rates. Dividends received are discounted to their
present value at purchase and accumulated as the holding
period increases. The higher the dividend yielding a stock,

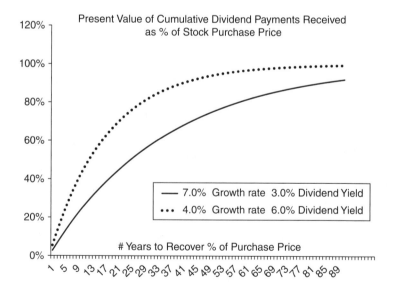

Figure 1.3   Dividend discount model.
Source: Author.

the faster it recovers its purchase price. The lower the dividend yield, the longer it takes to earn back the original cost price.

Interest-Rate Sensitivity

Stock prices are in general not insulated from changes in interest rates. A stock may produce dividend payments, but those are not always certain and they are not specified by a stated maturity. The term "terminal value" is for stocks less reliable than it is for bonds. A stock is a discounted cash flow of dividend payments, and therefore the term "present value" does apply in the same way as it does for bonds. When interest rates change, the present value of stocks can change. Historically, stocks have shown to be very sensitive to interest rate changes such as those in the 1970s and early 1980s. During those periods of sustained rise in interest rates, stocks in general did not perform well. Bonds did not perform during the 1970s and 80s so well either. A key difference between stocks and bonds is that the latter has a fixed coupon, which provides stability of regular payment. Bonds are also higher up in the capital structure of a company. That means in a liquidation or bankruptcy, corporate bond holders are likely to get their coupon paid before the stock holder gets its dividend. When a company issues corporate debt, it can impact its earnings positively when bonds are issued in a falling interest rate environment. That is because a lower cost of debt brings down a company's weighted average cost of capital. The result is that a company can use the favorable cost of capital to invest in new equipment or to buy back its shares. The buy-back of shares has been a trend that intensified since 2009. The S&P 500 Index companies have bought back their stock in greater numbers since 2009 and that has supported the broad market index. Having said that, while the level of the S&P 500 Index may matter, the reverse is true for earnings estimates and forward multiples. Their movements are driven by whether or not the Federal Reserve is hiking or cutting rates, and the earnings and multiples cycles often counteract one another.

Forward earnings estimates grow robustly when the Fed is hiking rates and fall when it begins to cut rates before expanding again, albeit at a slower pace than in the earlier stages. Multiples, on the other hand, expand considerably in stages when the Fed cuts, and contract sharply when the Fed starts to hike. In other words, the behavior of earnings estimates is procyclical – they rise much more when the Fed is hiking rates (trying to cool off a robust economy) than when it is cutting them (trying to rejuvenate a tepid one). Relative sector estimates respond in kind. Late cyclical stocks like Industrials and Materials rise the most when the Fed is hiking, and defensive stocks like Utilities hold up the best when the Fed begins cutting. Early cyclical stocks like Technology enjoy the biggest expansion when rate cuts continue after the federal funds rate is below a long run average. The behavior of earnings multiples is countercyclical and sector leadership realigns accordingly. Table 1.1 on page 20 shows the early cyclical stocks have the best of the multiple expansion in Phase I when the Fed hikes slowly, and share leadership with the defensives in Phase II when the Fed hikes quickly. This happens before the defensive stocks take over in Phase III (when the Fed cuts slowly). All of the late cyclical sectors' relative multiples expand in Phase IV, and they are the winners on balance from a multiples perspective when the Fed is easing quickly. This pattern broadly supports the notion that stocks are forward looking, beginning to discount the effects of policy moves before they occur.

Exploring past Phase IV and Phase I patterns provides some insight into what to expect for equities in the intermediate term, especially as the extraordinary easing measures by the Federal Reserve are slowly wound down. Historically, when the two-year Treasury yield bottoms, it seems to have a good record of leading peaks in the overall S&P 500 price-to-earnings multiple. This pattern has held across Phase IVs for the early cyclical sectors (see Table 1.1 on page 20), just as the reverse (higher yields lead to higher multiples) has held for the late cyclical stocks and technology. Another way in which this dynamic can be seen is in the tendency of early cyclical stock earnings multiples to peak well ahead of the end of Phase IV (the phase the Fed cuts quickly). Health care's relative multiple, on the other hand, has steadily declined across all of Phase IV. The rest of the defensive sectors' multiple histories during Phase IV are mixed.

Interest-rate sensitivity is measured by duration. Duration is the weighted-average term to maturity of a bond's cash flows, and measures its price sensitivity to changes in interest rates. Duration drives capital gains in the fixed-income market. There have been academic attempts to extend the concept of duration to equities, but with little success. Equities expressed as a discounted stream of dividend payments represent a good example of a cross-over characteristic with bonds. Unlike the coupon, however, the dividend is variable and perhaps better compared with a floating-rate note [FRN] that earns variable interest as a spread over a reference index (typically the London Interbank Offer Rate Index [LIBOR]). A floating-rate security has little duration however. Equity duration, however, in the context of the discount dividend model sees common estimates of around 20 to 30 years based on the long history

Table 1.1 Returns of different sectors versus changes in Fed interest rates

S&P 500 Individual Index average performance

	Consumer	Financials	Energy	Industrials	Materials	Utilities	Technology
Phase I: Fed hiked slowly (1997, 1999–00, 2004–06 cycles)	8%	–2%	30%	18%	9%	–10%	12%
Phase II: Fed hiked quickly (1980–81, 1983–84, 1988–89, 1993–94 cycles)	–7%	–6%	3%	9%	–6%	–7%	–2%
Phase III: Fed cut slowly (1996 cycle)	11%	31%	21%	22%	–1%	5%	4%
Phase IV: Fed cut quickly (2007–08 cycle)	–18%	–28%	19%	4%	3.80%	15%	10%

Source: FRBNY. Annual data from 1990–2014.

of dividend policy from major blue chip companies. In contrast to the contractually established schedule of bond-holder payments, cash streams accruing to stockholders are not predictable and therefore not stable. The relation-ship between rates and equity security valuations weakens when additional variables driving credit and equity prices make themselves felt. Such variables are default, earnings misses, or corporate governance. While duration facili-tates the comparison of interest-rate sensitivities across bonds, providing a quantitative basis for hedging interest-rate exposure within a fixed-income portfolio, it serves lit-tle function in a stock portfolio. Historically, stocks with the highest dividend payout ratios exhibit negative cor-relations with interest rates. They tend to underperform the broader market when rates are rising, and outperform when rates fall. The negative correlations for those divi-dend stocks are seen as a sign that the market views them as proxies for bonds.

There are several prominent examples of proxies for bonds. These are real-estate investment trusts (REITs), Telecoms, and Utilities. These companies face tight regulatory constraints that limit their earnings potential, and much of these stocks' total returns come from stable dividends. The impact of rela-tive reliance on dividends to satisfy shareholder returns are, for example, Household Products, Hypermarkets, Packaged Foods, Soft Drinks, and Tobacco. Sectors that are positively correlated with interest-rate changes include Casinos, Construction and Engineering, Health-Care Facilities, Internet Software and Services, and Life Sciences. These sec-tors are shown in Table 1.2 on page 22.

The data in Table 1.2 show that most sectors' performance has a directly related return to interest rates. In general, investing in high-dividend payout-ratio stocks implies a

Table 1.2 Sector performance relative to the S&P 500 Index

	Rising Rates	Falling Rates
Pharmaceuticals	−60%	50%
Electric Utilities	−62%	69%
Health–care Equipment	−6%	9%
Soft Drinks	−53%	59%
Hypermarkets	−71%	78%
Packaged Foods & Meats	−35%	47%
Tobacco	−16%	110%
Household Products	−55%	52%

Source: FRB, 1971–2014. *Performance of sector relative to S&P 500. Periods are selected during rising rate periods (1980–1982, 1994, 1999, 2004–06) and falling rates periods (1995–1998, 2007–08, 2010–2011, 2014).

reliance on current income and an accompanying elevated sensitivity to changes in interest rates. That sensitivity may at times attract investor flows to high dividend-paying stocks from bonds when interest rates fall. In case interest rates rise however, those stock funds may experience outflows. Bonds and dividend-paying stocks are therefore not perfect substitutes, especially for investors who value capital appreciation over current income. Earnings have a level of cyclicality, and stocks that experience earnings variability exert a meaningful influence on the interest-rate sensitivity of the overall portfolio. The greater the cyclicality of earnings, the more likely the aggregate stock price is to be positively correlated with interest rates. Using the variability of earnings estimates over time as a proxy for earnings cyclicality, the variability can serve as a robust predictor of directional sensitivity to interest rates. All eight of the industry groups shown in Table 1.2 demonstrated consistent underperformance versus the S&P 500 Composite Index when rates rose and outperformance when interest rates fell. Sectors like Airlines, Health Care Supplies and the composite REIT industry group failed to demonstrate consistent relative performance when their stock prices are positively correlated with rate changes. The empirical link between earnings cyclicality and interest-rate sensitivity is especially strong among several of the subindustries within the Materials and Utilities sector.

S&P 500 earnings multiples have demonstrated a robust positive correlation with real interest rates except at extremely low and high levels of real rates. In an economy characterized by widespread disinflationary influences, interest rate changes may serve as a robust leading indicator of growth prospects, reinforcing the robustness of the link between earnings cyclicality and interest rate. The level of long-term real interest rates has a relationship with the PE multiple. In periods when the multiple expands, real interest rates rise and are positive. That is a sign of a strong economy with healthy earnings. When real interest rates are negative, PE multiples may expand, but that could be a sign of a weak economy when companies slash costs to keep positive earnings. Figure 1.4 shows

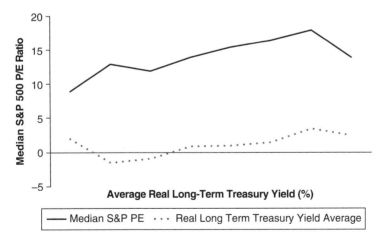

Figure 1.4 S&P median PE multiple in periods of high and low real interest rates.

Source: Robert Shiller: 1971–2014.

the long-term relationship between real interest rates and the PE multiple.

Equity Returns

The universe of financial securities (stocks, bonds, currencies, commodities, and cash equivalents) derives returns from the performance of the real economy. The real economy is driven by various factors like capital, labor, materials, and productivity. These factors determine gross domestic product (GDP), and GDP growth is the ultimate source of all cash flows and returns across the capital structure of financial assets. There has been a historical relationship between equities and productivity growth. Within the universe of assets, stocks are an asset class that reflects the upside potential of productivity. The reason for this is because corporate profit margins are the residual of the costs of labor, capital, raw materials, and credit. A quantitative measure of equity risk and return is historical performance. Figure 1.5 on page 25 shows historical returns and return volatilities of bonds and stocks over the past 100 years.

During this long period, the risk and return profiles were uneven across both assets. Lower volatility assets, such as cash alternatives and Treasury bonds, provided low upside and low downside within a relatively symmetric distribution. Higher volatility assets such as stocks provided more upside than downside during short-term periods. To take history at face value, total returns on equity can be decomposed into three distinct factors: income return (dividend), growth return (GDP and earnings), and valuation returns (changes in PE ratios). The returns from income are the lower volatility aspect of equity return. It is mainly driven by two subcomponents, which is the cash flow from dividends, and the cash flow from gross repurchases of outstanding shares.

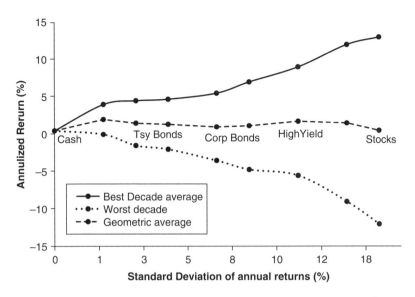

Figure 1.5 Historical returns between stocks and bonds over different periods.

Source: Ibbotson, Shiller. Period 1900–2011, annual data.

It is important to distinguish, however, whether returns from income comes from the use of financial leverage or from earnings retention. Returns from GDP and earnings growth are also driven by two factors. The most important factor is nominal GDP. The relationship between nominal GDP growth and earnings growth is fairly consistent over longer periods (up to 20 years). The third component is the return from valuation changes. Over the long term, equity prices have tended to keep pace with earnings. This has given equity valuations a mean-reverting character.

In his book *Irrational Exuberance* (2000), Robert Shiller derived the "cyclically adjusted P/E multiple" with these three return components. This ratio describes earnings as being volatile (historically, earnings are twice as volatile as equity prices). Stock prices derive their valuation from those volatile earnings. Thus, a cyclical adjustment is useful in removing volatility from earnings. Shiller uses a trailing ten-year average of reported earnings as a cyclically adjusted portion of the PE ratio. When taking the three major components (GDP, PE ratio and dividend), equity total returns can be expressed as the following sum:

1. stock index dividend yield
2. percent change in nominal GDP
3. percent change in profits' share of GDP
4. percent change in cyclically adjusted P/E ratio
5. percent change in real long-term Treasury yield

To calculate equity total returns, a fundamental discounting factor should be included which has generally been defined as the return on a long-term government bond. When considering components 1 through 5 above as the main sources for equity return, a simple comparison is the S&P 500 earnings per share and US nominal GDP in dollars. Figure 1.6 shows the two series track each other

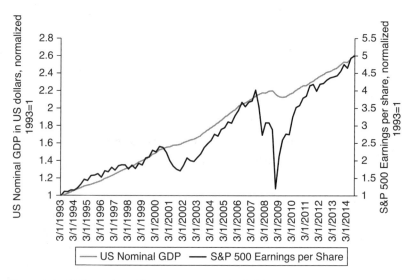

Figure 1.6   S&P earnings/share versus nominal GDP.
Source: Robert Shiller, data 1993–2014.

relatively closely. The close trend between GDP and S&P 500 earnings explains that nominal GDP is ultimately the key source for long-term expected returns.

Bond Returns

A yield on a bond can be decomposed as the sum of the following: expectations of the path of future short-term interest rates, and a risk premium for bearing uncertainty, known as the term premium. Historically, bond returns can be broken down into three components:

- returns resulting from change in economic growth
- returns resulting from change in inflation
- returns resulting from change in the term premium

A bond return is closely related to the expectations of a short-term rate, such as the federal funds rate. The third component is a residual after growth and inflation-related return expectations are subtracted from the bond's total expected return. Historically, a ten-year maturity US Treasury bond has returned around 5 percent annually. When the three components are stripped out, 0.5 percent is attributed to economic growth, represented by the long-term real return on three-month Treasury bills. There is about 3 percent of the ten-year yield that is accounted for change in inflation as measured by the consumer price index (CPI) index, and about 1.25 percent is contributed by the term premium. This is the excess return on ten-year US Treasury bond after accounting for the real returns on T-bills and inflation. The most critical component of bonds' total return is the real policy rate. The real policy rate has been on average around 0.4 percent since the 1900s, rising as high as 5 percent in 1933 and falling as low as –6 percent in 1951. Today, the real

policy rate stands at around –1.25 percent (The fed funds
rate minus the CPI year-over-year growth rate). The path of
the real policy rate has historically been too low when the
rate was below fundamental fair value, which is known as
the "neutral rate." There have been other times when the
real policy rate was well above the neutral rate, like in the
1980s. The neutral rate has been subject to intense debate
by both academics and market participants. In general, the
neutral rate can be determined when real policy rates are
too low relative to their fundamental fair value and that
results in the acceleration of inflation. When the real policy
rate is too high relative to fundamental fair value, a deceler-
ation of real growth below potential growth may occur. The
basic forecast assumes there is a linear relationship between
the real policy rate approximated by the Treasury bill yield
adjusted for inflation, and the potential real growth rate of
the economy, as shown in Figure 1.7.

The historical path of the real policy rate has not been
optimal at all times. In the 1930s, it appeared that the

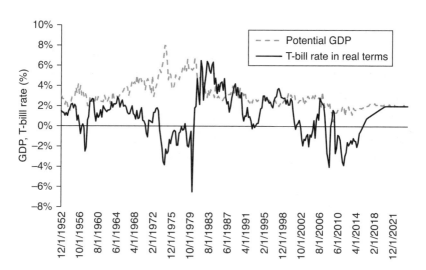

Figure 1.7   T-bill rate and potential GDP.
Source: FRB, Congressional Budget Office, 1952–2014, quarterly data.

real policy rate should have been falling to a negative rate instead of actually rising to a positive rate. And in the 1950s, it appeared that the policy rate should have been rising to a positive rate instead of actually falling to a negative rate. Barring those two periods, it appears that the generally the relationship between potential GDP growth and the real policy rate has held, and continues to do so today. There is a macroeconomic debate behind the policy rate over the long term. The debate was sparked by "secular stagnation," which became a popular topic in the media and among several economists, like Krugman and Lawrence Summers. Secular stagnation is caused by low demand stemming from deleveraging and tight credit. The resulting output gap and slack are large and exert downward pressure on nominal wages and inflation. The path of short-term interest rates remains near zero for an extended time. The policy rate can only return to equilibrium when the output gap is fully closed. In the event that the economy faces a supply-side problem, it is caused by demographics, a falling labor force participation rate, and low capital investment. The output gap is smaller, inflation pressure can start to build, and rates hikes may follow sooner. However, because of lower potential output and lower returns on capital, the policy rate eventually ends at a lower neutral rate.

By late 2006, the Fed acknowledged something had changed in US potential output. The Fed staff forecast a slower labor force growth because of looming baby boom retirement. That implied that the expansion of potential GDP could be lower than what was witnessed in the earlier 2000s. The subsequent downward shift in potential GDP since the 2008 crisis was coupled with an acceleration in early retirement. With potential GDP settling at a more permanent lower level, the Federal Open Market Committee (FOMC) has incorporated into its forecasts a number of structural factors that have contributed to a persistent decline in interest rates, such as global savings, demographic changes, slower potential GDP, and fiscal and credit restraints. A downward shift in potential growth as a result of these factors means the equilibrium between aggregate demand and supply has equally moved down. This has led to a debate on what the level equilibrium policy rate could be. There are a number of different ideas about how the "equilibrium real interest rate" can be established. A school of thought is the equilibrium rate is the required rate of return to keep an economy's output near potential. Potential output represents the sum of population, labor force participation, and productivity growth. A deviation by actual output from potential is a direct measure of future change in employment and inflation. The rise or fall of actual output versus potential has therefore a level of speed driven by inflation expectations. The equilibrium real return that approximates the speed is the "ex ante real interest rate." This ex ante rate is the nominal rate minus long-term inflation expectations. The developed economies are likely suffering from a combination of supply and demand constraints. In overlevered, highly indebted economies, the equilibrium real rate is also a measure of an interest rate that stabilizes large debt to GDP. This rate is a function of how the cyclically adjusted primary balance relates to debt to GDP and real GDP. In order to forecast what the level of the real policy rate may be in the next decade, there is a set of assumptions to take into account. These assumptions are: (1) potential GDP growth in the United States will gradually decline from a 2 percent rate today, to a 1.5 percent rate by 2023; (2) US debt-to-GDP ratio will broadly stabilize at today's levels of around 100 percent; (3) realized inflation will broadly follow market expectations expressed in the inflation-linked bond market.

Under these assumptions, the real policy rate may potentially average –1 percent per annum for the next decade, and if there are no major changes to the assumptions beyond that, actually fall gradually toward –1.25 percent by 2030. Against this secular forecast, the market expected in 2014–2015 the real policy rate to rise from –1.3 percent to about –0.6 percent by 2023, and to a positive 0.6 percent by 2030. Assuming the forecast for the secular horizon of the "optimal" real policy rate is correct, and assuming inflation follows the path of market expectations, the bond market may deliver positive expected returns for the decade ahead (excluding any exogenous shocks). If policymakers follow the optimal path of secular real policy rates from this point forward, the ten-year US Treasury note (a proxy for the bond market) can be expected to deliver an average total return of about 2.0 percent to 3.0 percent per annum over the next five to ten years. Further, an expectation of –1 percent real policy rates, combined with 2.5 percent expected inflation, produces a risk-neutral fair value yield of 1.5 percent for ten-year US Treasuries. Given that the current yield at time writing was around 2 percent to 2.5 percent, the term premium is determined to be 1 percent below its long-term average.

There is a word of caution about the assumptions and interest rate forecast. History taught one lesson, and that is policymakers often make mistakes either due to regime changes or because of observational errors. Although there is broad confidence in the FOMC following the historically derived optimal path of real policy rates, there remain concerns that either external currency pressures and/or domestic political pressures might cause a deviation from the prescribed lower-for-longer path. As has been the case historically, the errors in suboptimal policy are likely to be repeated in generally the same way. The result of a too high real policy rate path relative to the one prescribed by historical optimization will undoubtedly be a sharp rise in private defaults given the historically high debt/GDP ratios with which we are confronted today. Conversely, the result of a too low real policy rate path relative to the one prescribed by historical optimization will likely be a more rapid erosion of confidence in the US dollar as a sustainable global reserve currency, sparking financial and then real deglobalization, leading to economic stagflation.

Other Valuation Metrics: Tobin's Q and Equity-Bond Risk Premium

When theory is applied in practice, the observed reality can be different from derived reality. Portfolio balance theory is such an example. It promises future returns by exchanging assets. An important measure of portfolio balance is Tobin's Q ratio. This is the ratio of the price of existing asset prices relative to the marginal cost of producing new assets. Whenever the ratio is below one, companies are undervalued because new businesses cannot be created as cheaply as where they would be trading in the market. The Q ratio tends to mean revert near one and has done so since quantitative easing began in 2009. At that time, the ratio was at its lowest since the 1950s, as shown in Figure 1.8 on page 33.

Today's ratio stood at 1.15 in 2014, and in Tobin's view an above parity suggests deploying real assets will earn a sufficient future rate of return. The reason for this is that the replacement cost of producing new assets is likely sufficient to regenerate today's returns. When the Q ratio is below one, as was the case from 2008 to 2013, investors have had to accept a discount to the replacement value if they desired to sell their assets. When the market-wide Q ratio is less than parity, investors are probably pessimistic about future asset returns. Because those returns expectations

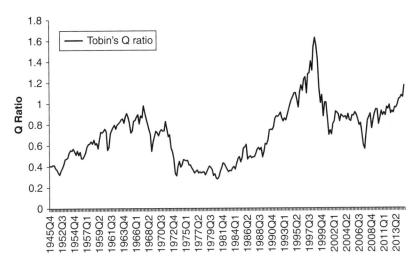

Figure 1.8   Tobin's Q.

Source: Federal Reserve Z.1 Financial Accounts of the United States, H.4 reserve balances
Q ratio: nonfinancial corporations' value/nonfinancial corporations' replacement cost
(residential/nonresidential).

lower future expected values, those expectations question
the assumptions behind existing assets relative to their
marginal production cost. The cost would have to be low-
ered in order to get broader investment. In the "theory" of
Tobin, this can only be achieved by changing expectations
about future discount rates. When this is done appropriately, it changes the rate of returns on existing and future
assets, thereby creating new supply of assets. Because there
is a given demand for those new assets, replacement costs
will fall again relative to market values. If that is the case,
it will presumably move Tobin's Q over 1, suggesting an
investment cycle may commence, which seemed to be the
case in 2014, albeit corporate capital expenditure plan sur-
veys pointed at caution. In Tobin's work, expected interest
rates are a function of demand for cash and bonds. When
expected interest rates exceed current interest rates, there
will be more demand for cash than for bonds (vice versa).

Different types of investors set different expected rate of
returns. In order not to have those returns deviate too
materially, Tobin suggested that assets need to be substitut-
able in order to change expected returns. The return that is
achieved over the life of a bond investment is the coupon
interest discounted by the yield to maturity. The yield to
maturity, however, fluctuates because it resembles a sum of
expectations that change frequently.

These expectations range from what investors see as future
inflation, where they expect short-term interest rates to
be, and what they think is the "term premium." The term
premium is the extra return investors demand for holding a longer maturity bond. According to the expectations
hypothesis, the term premium is the same as the expected
return from rolling over a series of short-maturity bonds with
a total maturity equal to that of a long-maturity bond. In
other words, investors require compensation across the term
structure of interest rates, the yield curve. The further out
on the yield curve, the more expectations express a greater
uncertainty about the trajectory of inflation, and the less
clarity there is about the path of short-term interest rates.
The term premium is also demanded as compensation for
volatility and liquidity. The liquidity preference theory says
that short-term securities are less risky, and as a result, yield
curves have an invariably small, positively sloped "tail" on
the far left side. At this part of the curve, investors would be
willing to give up some liquidity premium in exchange for
investing in longer maturity securities. Interest rate options
provide information on parts of the yield curve that exhibit
higher excess returns because of localized higher volatility.

The Federal Reserve has published a model that estimates
the term premium. The researchers, Don Kim and Jonathan
Wright, employ a three-factor model that uses the level of
interest rates, the slope, and curvature of the yield curve. At

each major point of the curve—two-year, five-year, and ten-year maturity—the residual value (term premium) is calculated after adjusting for long-term inflation expectations and expected real short-term interest rates. What can be concluded from Figure 1.9 is that term premiums have been falling over the last 20 years as interest rate tightening cycles became further spread out and interest rate volatility fell. The term premium can experience sudden sharp changes. For example, when in May 2013 Fed chairman Bernanke indicated asset purchases could be slowed in the foreseeable future, markets quickly demanded a higher term premium—dubbed as the "taper tantrum." This tantrum was caused predominately by a shift in perceptions the Federal Reserve would maintain near-zero interest rates and asset purchases for an "indefinite" period of time. Even so, the term premium remains well below the historical average of 1 percent, and currently stands at 0 percent, according to the Fed's Kim-Wright model.

The low value of the term premium was addressed by Bernanke in his speech from March 2006, titled "Reflections on the Yield Curve and Monetary Policy." Bernanke noted

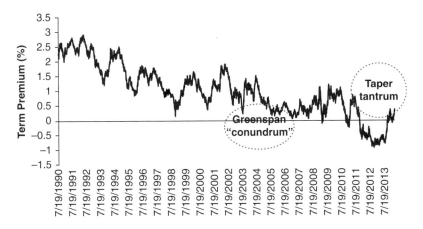

Figure 1.9 US ten-year Treasury term premium.

Source: Federal Reserve Board, Don H. Kim and Jonathan H. Wright (2005, 2013). Data: daily, July 1990-March 31, 2014.

the fall in the term premium in 2004–2006 was attributed to several factors, such as reduced macroeconomic volatility, stable long-term inflation expectations, recycling of dollar reserves by foreign official institutions, a change in pension fund accounting toward long-term asset-liability matching, and a fall in the issuance of long-term securities. In a follow-up speech, titled "Long Term Interest Rates," which was delivered at the Annual Monetary Conference in San Francisco in March 2013, Bernanke showed that the term premium had fallen to a negative value during 2011–2012. This phenomenon may occur during times of heightened uncertainty when safe have demand for longer maturity Treasury securities dominates. The Fed's asset purchase programs and Operation Twist also had an influence on the level of the term premium. In a separate study that was posted on the New York Fed blog Liberty Street Economics in August 2013, research staffers Adrian and Fleming demonstrated that the sell-off in interest rates during May–August 2013 was largely caused by the term premium that saw a greater change than during the 2003 or 1994 long-term interest rate rises. The term premium therefore matters to policymakers and financial markets. During 2004–2006, low term premiums were dubbed a "conundrum" because the rise in short-term interest rates barely changed the level of long-term interest rates. Central bank forward guidance that continues to anchor the shorter end of the yield has a similar effect on likely maintaining a downward bias on long-term term premiums.

The equity risk premium is the excess return that an individual stock or the overall stock market provides over a "risk-free rate." A way to calculate this is to use the reciprocal of the P/E ratio of the stock index and subtract a risk-free rate, a Treasury bill, or a Treasury bond yield. Numerous studies have compared long-term returns between stocks and bonds.

Academics such as Robert Shiller and Robert Ibbotson have researched extensively associated equity and market risk premiums. A simple conclusion from this research can be drawn: equities always outperform bonds over the long run, albeit with periods of extreme volatility. To visualize, one way to show this holds true is to look at the historical real earnings yield of the S&P 500 Index and at long-term Treasury yield, adjusted for annual inflation. Historically, long bond real yields have averaged around 4.5 percent, and the equity real earnings yield has been around 6.9 percent. The gap between the two is known as the "equity risk premium." The equity risk premium is shown in Figure 1.10 on page 38. To compare expected returns between "safe haven" bonds such as Treasuries and stock returns, the "cyclically adjusted PE ratio" used by Shiller may provide additional insight. This PE ratio uses a trailing ten-year average of reported earnings to smooth out their cyclical volatility (earnings can be twice as volatile as the equity prices). Based on Shiller's most recent estimate, the cyclically adjusted PE ratio stood around 26 versus 18 for the actual ratio of the S&P 500 Index by early 2015. Projected five years forward, the compounded annual growth rate (CAGR) of the cyclically adjusted PE ratio is 7.5 percent, adjusted for annual inflation. This number presents a forward return on the broader stock index that may not necessarily materialize. But it does say that, based on low interest rates, the excess return premium demanded on stocks is higher than on bonds. For example, from 1945 to 1970, when real interest rates were on average 2 percent negative, the average historical CAGR five years and ten years projected forward of the PE ratio were around 4 percent adjusted for inflation. That CAGR equal to an excess premium of 4 percent is about similar to the recent period of 2008 to 2014 when real interest rates were also negative 1 percent to 2 percent. The historical comparison between

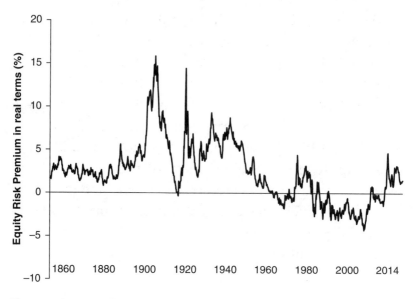

Figure 1.10 Equity risk premium.
Source: Robert Shiller, 1860–2014, quarterly data.

the two periods may suggest a few things. On the one hand, negative real interest rates can generate higher PE multiples when free cash flow improves because of a lower discount rate. On the other hand, PE multiple expansions may also happen because of uncertainty that results in lower (real) interest rates. In each case, the equity risk premium is likely to be positive (see Figure 1.10).

When Equity Is Like Debt and Debt Is Like Equity

There are numerous of examples of a cross-over between stocks and bonds. The cross-over becomes most evident when a stock has embedded bond features or a bond has equity characteristics. A good example is the "convertible bond." This is a bond the holder can convert into a specified number of shares of common stock in the issuing company or cash of equal value. It is a hybrid security with debt- and equity features. Convertible bonds were originated in the mid-nineteenth century, and used by early speculators to counter market cornering. Convertible bonds are often issued by companies with a low credit rating and high growth potential. To compensate for having additional value through the option of converting the bond to stock, a convertible bond typically has a coupon rate lower than that of similar, nonconvertible debt. The investor receives the potential upside of conversion into equity, while protecting the downside with cash flow from the coupon payments and the return of principal upon maturity. These properties lead naturally to the idea of convertible arbitrage, in which a long position in the convertible bond is balanced by a short position in the underlying equity.

Another way to spot cross-over opportunities is to look at the correlation between high-yield, hybrid, senior unsecured, corporate, and subordinated debt, and a company's stock or broader equity index. The reason why there is a positive correlation is due to the placement in the hierarchy of the capital structure. High-yield and subordinated debt are at the lower end of the capital structure, closer to the equity holders who are at the bottom. The rank order exists because of bankruptcy codes or regulatory reasons, such as the "bail-in" mechanism. That mechanism has been put in place in Europe to have bond- and equity holders partially pay for the bailout of a failed bank. This has not always been the case, however. During the 2008 banking crisis, traditional hybrid and subordinated debt was frequently unable to absorb the losses of failed entities, with the consequence that governments had to step in and recapitalize banks at the taxpayer's expense. Contingent convertible capital notes ("CoCos") were the industry's response to both the needs of the banks and investors' requirements for a larger capital base without diluting shareholders' equity. Contingent convertible capital instruments are loss-absorbing hybrid securities issued by banks. They are debt obligations that either convert into equity or allow principal to be written down, often at a predefined capital trigger. Once converted or written-down, CoCos fully absorb capital without triggering the bank's default. There are further examples of cross-over-type instruments such as hybrid securities, and convertible coupon step-up notes. The reason for cross-over between bonds and stock is often mentioned in the context of credit risk. In that regard, even government bonds from time to time correlate positively with equity risk. It is important to understand why there is a positive correlation and how that might change. Earning a return on an individual stock or bond can be an absolute matter. Investors who want earn a coupon or dividend may not want to consider active cross-over investing in stocks and bonds. Cross-over investing in stocks and bonds is strategic and dynamic. Most important is to identify which specific stocks and bonds are a natural "pick" to maximize returns.

Crossing over the Pickers

The ability to successfully select the best bond and the best stock is what differentiates the consistently effective picker. In 2008, Bill Miller stepped down from the Legg Mason Value Trust fund, which he had managed for 30 years. In the five years since the streak ended, Miller's fund lost 9 percent annually and ranked last out of the 840 funds in its category, according to Lipper. The reason for his spectacular crash after his equally spectacular run was that his winning streak was so extraordinary because Miller was an impressive stock picker. A newsletter published by Credit Suisse-First Boston in 2003, a few years before Miller's winning streak ended, calculated the odds of a manager's outperforming the market on chance alone for 12 straight years to be one in 2.2 billion. Some would say that Miller's ability to pick the right stocks was merely a coin toss. If Miller was singled out at the start of 1991 and calculated the odds that by pure chance the specific fund manager selected would beat the market for precisely the next 15 years, then those odds would indeed have been astronomically low.

On the other side of the investment spectrum stood Bill Gross, the astute bond investor who beat the Barclays Aggregate Bond Index from 1987 up until 2011. Gross was and still *is* a superb bond picker. His ability to see value within the fixed-income universe was based on basic principles of a total return approach to bonds. By 2011, the market challenged his approach because of high uncertainty and central bank action that drove US Treasury yields lower and strengthened the dollar. Both factors led to falling emerging market currencies and bonds, and a flatter Treasury yield curve. The rise and fall of a stock/bond picker may also be explained by the historical returns of active fund managers. According to ICI Mutual Fund research, for the past 20-year period (1994–2014), active equity investors earned 3.83 percent and asset allocation fund investors earned 2.56 percent (after fees) compared to the S&P 500 return of 9.14 percent. For the same period, fixed-income investors earned 1.01 percent compared to the Barclays Aggregate Bond Index return of 6.89 percent. The return differences can be explained by the fact that investors diligently seek investments that they hope will produce the best returns, but lose much of that benefit when they yield to psychological factors. Investors who limit the time retention for investments erode the alpha created by professional investment management. The average equity investor earned an annualized return that outpaced inflation for both the twenty-year and the one-year time frames. Fixed-income and asset allocation investors continue to lose ground to inflation as their investments lag the cost of living in all but the exceptional one-year time frame. History shows that mutual fund investors generally increase inflows after observing periods of strong performance. They buy at high prices when future expected returns are lower, and they sell after observing periods of poor performance when future expected returns are now higher. This results in what author Carl Richards called the "behavior gap," in which investor returns are well below the returns of the funds in which they invest. Perhaps with this observation in mind, Warren Buffett once said, "The most important quality for an investor is temperament, not intellect" (The Motley Fool, 2014). That statement says that stock- or bond picking is a way to consistently outperform.

This book addresses the methods of picking bonds and applies those methods to picking stocks. The chapters in this book focus on how to use bond strategies to enhance stock-picking strategies. The same analysis is applied to equity strategy to identify value in individual bonds. The approach is a relative value concept as opposed to a deep-value or fundamental analysis. The book does not argue that by using fixed-income strategies, a stock investor is guaranteed to outperform. The same can be said for a bond investor using equity strategy to enhance returns. Every investor makes her or his own judgment as to why a stock or a bond has value or why it has not. This book's purpose is to help investors understand different selection methods by analyzing and presenting practical cases of individual selection. The following chapters devote bottoms up analysis, relative value frameworks and ideas on cross-over opportunities between stocks and bonds. The author of the book hopes the investor can apply some of the presented techniques to her or his asset allocation strategy to further optimize his or her portfolios.

2

Fixed-Income Strategies for the Equity Investor

In fixed-income investing and bond trading, "picking" always played an important role. Picking individual bonds relative to an index or on a stand-alone basis can make a difference in earning excess return on a bond portfolio. Bonds are, therefore, with regard to the asset allocation process and individual security selection, not too dissimilar from stocks. Bonds are, however, mathematically very different from stocks. To be a good bond or stock picker requires an eye for the underlying detail that supports the decision to buy or sell a bond or a stock. There are number of ways to pick a bond. The following sections provide frameworks for how to look at bond picking and how to incorporate such methods into picking stocks.

A Carry Framework

Bonds earn a fixed or floating rate coupon from which a yield can be derived by discounting the coupons over a certain term. Bonds may look at face value boring as all that the investor would do is "clipping coupons." That is not always true, however. The coupon and yield of a bond provide an income that is called "carry." Carry is the difference between the coupon and the interest earned on cash, say, interest on a deposit. The carry is therefore a trade-off.

Either an investor is willing to take some risk by investing in a bond or he keeps his liquidity in cash by earning a lower interest rate. The carry can also be calculated as the difference between the coupon and a "repo rate." The repo rate is the rate of interest at which bonds can be financed by lending or borrowing them as collateral in money markets. From a financing perspective, stocks also have a carry component. A stock can be financed on margin at the stock exchange. Alternatively, a stock's dividend yield can be compared to where a company funds in the commercial paper market. Another way would be to subtract a company's corporate debt yield from it's stock's earning yield (reciprocal of the Price to Earnings ratio). The carry premium can also be calculated by analyzing the "free cash flow yield". The free cash flow yield is expressed as the ratio of free cash flow divided by company's market value. The stock's carry can be calculated by taking the difference between the free cash flow yield and a company's cost of debt or commercial paper yield. In comparing the free cash flow, dividend or earnings yield with a company's financing rate, "carry" as it is commonly used in fixed income, may not be too different for stocks. Only the "stability" of carry is different. Bonds and stocks represent a discounted cash flow. However, a coupon is fixed over the life of the bonds unless otherwise stated (for example, floating rate securities). A stock's dividend yield, cash flow yield, or earnings yield is not fixed and may experience variability. In addition, a dividend, cash flow, or earnings yield is a ratio rather than a fixed percentage. Therefore "carry" in the traditional sense of bonds based on comparing coupon interest versus a funding rate has more stability than carry from a stock based on comparing dividend, free cash flow or earnings yield to shorter term financing.

A carry return can also be calculated in other ways. For example, carry can be earned from taking a position in a foreign currency. If an investor were to buy a bond denominated in a foreign currency, then in addition to the bond's total return (coupon interest plus principal and potential price appreciation), the short-term interest-rate differential implied from the currency could be an additional source of return. A currency's value is predominantly determined by the interest-rate differential between the home country and a foreign country. Many companies issue bonds denominated in different currencies. Companies do this to take advantage of interest-rate differences as well as getting access to liquidity provided by foreign investors and financial intermediaries. Multicurrency issuance can also be applied to stocks. Many multinational companies have their shares traded on domestic and foreign stock exchanges, or they are issued as American depository receipts (ADRs) to list shares. An ADR is a negotiable certificate issued by a US bank representing a specified number of shares in a foreign stock that is traded on a US exchange. For an investor to take advantage of a mismatch in share valuation of company, a currency valuation model may be effective. Currencies may exhibit volatility, however, that at times negates the positive return that can be earned from the interest-rate differential implied by the exchange rate. Investors can, however, benefit from additional "currency carry return" when selecting international stocks and bonds. Buying the stock of a company in a foreign currency that is undervalued relative to its stock listed in its home country could provide the potential of higher returns (although there are no guarantees).

Another source for carry return is credit risk. Credit risk can be measured by a company's credit rating provided by rating agencies like Standard and Poor's. Credit risk is also measured by a company's corporate bonds that are priced with an option-adjusted spread (OAS) over the comparable "risk free" Treasury bond yield. The OAS, known as the "credit spread", is wider when credit risk is higher. When credit risk rises, bonds and stocks can come close to each other in terms of price volatility and risk-adjusted returns. When comparing the OAS spread or yield of a company's corporate bond to the dividend yield of stock, it is a basic measure of capital structure valuation. When the yield on corporate debt is expressed as a ratio of the dividend yield, the investor can gauge whether corporate debt is over- or undervalued to the stock.

It is often said in the financial media that stocks reside at the "lower end of the capital structure." The capital structure is the sum of the amount of corporate debt and stock outstanding of a company. In practice that means that because stocks reside at the lower end of the capital structure, in case of a liquidation or bankruptcy, stockholders could get wiped out first. Equity holders therefore bear the greatest risk in the capital structure of a company. This is especially the case for companies that have a rating below investment grade, which is called "junk status." Those companies issue high-yield bonds and subordinated debt. Historically, the price volatility of newly issued high-yield and subordinated debt has not been too dissimilar from the volatility of stock prices. In that respect, high yield and subordinated debt are the closest linked to equity of a firm. When an investor wants to determine how bond valuation relates to stock valuation, the comparison between volatility of high yield debt and volatility of the stock can be another gauge.

An other way to compare bond volatility to stock volatility is to look at the credit risk premium on corporate debt. A higher credit risk premium on corporate debt may imply the earnings yield of a stock could be high as well (as a result of a lower Price to Earnings multiple). The reason is that when a company issues large amounts of debt, the credit risk premium should be higher. A company that uses higher leverage through debt issuance can also have bearing on earnings and thereby the price of the stock. The PE ratio could fall because of higher earnings as a result of leverage. That should result in a higher earnings yield on the stock and therefore provide potentially a higher equity carry return. There have also been cases in which companies that issue high-yield debt, pay a fairly high dividend yield on their stock. To find stocks with high carry, investors need to look at companies that issue a fair amount of high-yield debt. A greater weight of debt in the capital structure of company may also provide relative-value opportunities by comparing stock earning yields with high-yield debt returns. In that context, carry return is a comparison between a stock and corporate bond with a similar amount of price volatility.

A fixed-income investor looks for value in bonds on the yield curve. The yield curve is defined as the term structure of interest rates. A component of carry return that can be derived from the yield curve is called "roll down." The roll down comes from the slope of the yield curve. The slope is measured by the difference between yields on bonds with different maturities and the rate on overnight cash (short-term rate). If short-term interest rates do not fluctuate or change too much, an investor can capture the roll-down return by "sitting" on a bond for a certain period of time. In practice that means for example an investor purchased a bond with a five-year maturity that has a coupon/yield of 2 percent and a price at par (100). If a four-year maturity bond from the same issuer (or comparable issuer) is yielding 1.8 percent, then a roll-down return is 20 basis points (0.002 percent, the difference between the yield of a five-year and four-year maturity). The roll down return can be earned over the period of one year, provided the slope of the yield curve does not change materially. The total return would be calculated by multiplying the duration of the five-year maturity bond (that has 4.8 years of duration) times 20 basis points of the roll down return, plus the bond's yield of 2 percent. The total return would be approximately 3 percent, all else being equal. It is not a guaranteed return, but it is capital gain that can be collected over time if an investor is patient. The roll down return can be captured in almost any bond, provided short term interest rates are stable. To take the roll down return concept to stocks, it is quite differently applicable. It is difficult to imagine stocks having a yield curve. Stocks do not have a yield to maturity, and the only company-specific yield curve would be corporate debt issued at different maturities. For example, Apple and Verizon have issued corporate bonds with a maturity as short as one year and as long as thirty years. Let us think for a moment conceptually about the "equity yield curve." For example, a common stock trades at a different PE multiple than the preferred stock, convertible preferred, class A shares or class B shares, or its internationally issued stock. There would be different earning yields or free cash flow yields on each of these stocks of the same company. Comparing the earnings yield or free cash flow yield to locally issued debt would be the "carry return" of a stock. That would explain price differences between stocks of a company on different exchanges (which is also caused by foreign currency valuation). This is because the free cash flow yield (after subtracting the cost of debt) could be higher in a company's foreign market country versus its home market. One could also do this yield comparison by using dividend yields of companies that operate in the same sector and have similar activities.

There could be a "yield curve" of dividend, free cash flow and earning yields of different companies in the same sector. It is not a traditional term structure of yields like in fixed income. Rather, it is a "credit curve" that expresses the different risks between stocks on domestic and foreign stock exchanges. The risks would be liquidity, currency, and cost capital that can be lower overseas than at home due to favorable funding or taxation. However, unlike in bonds, an investor would not "sit on a stock" and earn a roll-down return. That is because the credit curve of stocks may not be upward sloping. The way a stock investor would earn "carry" would be through the average free cash flow yield derived from different parts of the world. That carry return is then the difference between the global free cash flow yield and the average global cost of capital derived from parts of the world in which a company may operate. The carry concept is based on looking at a yield curve as to how such is practiced in fixed income. The yield curve carry is likely most applicable to multinational companies that have overseas operations and stocks listed on foreign exchanges.

There is another way to capture carry from the yield curve. This technique is called "laddering." An investor would purchase several bonds with a different maturity rather than one bond with a single maturity. The sizing of the ladder portfolio is most important. Instead of putting all of the investable money into one bond, the ladder portfolio sizes appropriately the total notional investment across different maturities. This is an effective way of minimizing interest-rate risk and enhancing the liquidity profile of the portfolio. Typically the bonds' maturity dates are evenly spaced across several months or several years. That means, when bonds are maturing, the proceeds are reinvested at regular intervals and the prevailing market rate. When liquidity needs rise, the preference is to have bond maturities. The strategy reduces the reinvestment risk associated with rolling over maturing bonds into similar fixed-income products all at once. It also helps manage the flow of money, ensuring a steady stream of cash flows throughout the year.

In stocks, laddering is not a common strategy. That is not to say the technique cannot be applied to stocks. The bond ladder is a strategy that does not express a view on the direction of interest rates on daily basis. The ladder is about maximizing income with the highest efficiency to generate liquidity. This approach can be applied to regular paying dividend stocks that have dividend dates spread out. Laddering in that context is also about achieving a stable dividend reinvestment return. A stock ladder of companies that have stable dividends and free cash flow would become a diversification tool through the reinvesting of dividend proceeds from one stock into a different stock. The risk is, however, that the diversification is negated by unstable dividends. Hence, unlike in fixed income, in which a ladder is stable because of fixed coupons, an investor in stock should be more careful constructing a ladder strategy to ensure the selection of individual stocks have stable dividend payouts.

Laddering during an initial public offering (IPO) by purchasing shares at a given price is known as "price support." That means, other investors must also agree to purchase additional shares but at a higher price. The effect is the stock price gets artificially inflated, while insiders have the opportunity to buy the stock at the lower price. A lower price guarantees they will be able to sell at a higher price in the near future. This manipulation of stock prices has been under significant investigation. A different way of laddering is when some institutional investors are allocated shares at the IPO offer price both before and after secondary trading has started. It is assumed that allocations (plus secondary market purchases) exceed optimal holdings and that the lead investment bank can control the offloading of excessive shares in the secondary market. Controlling additional purchases and the sale of shares by specific investors allows the lead investment bank to respond optimally, on behalf of the issuer, to the arrival of informed secondary market investors. Approaching a stock portfolio with this ladder has been deemed illegal and subject to investigations.

Perhaps the most predominant source of carry in bonds is duration. Macauley duration is the weighted average time until cash flows are received, and is measured in years. This metric named after its creator, Frederick Macauley, who in 1938 published an article titled "The Movements of Interest Rates, Bond Yields and Stock Prices" for the National Bureau of Economic Research. Modified duration is the name given to price sensitivity, and is the percentage change in price for a unit change in yield. Generally, when one values and analyzes equities, interest rates can be an important factor. There is a direct link between the value of a stock and the short-term interest rate. Hence, stocks should theoretically also have a first derivative in price sensitivity in relation to the short-term interest rate. In a dividend discounting model, the change in value of a stock is completely determined by the growth in the dividends that the stock will pay in the future. If you estimate the growth in dividend yield by a certain rate, the value of the price of a stock is its dividend amount divided by the difference between the interest rate and growth rate, shown by the formula below.

$$P = \frac{D}{r - g}.$$

In order to calculate the interest rate sensitivity, in other words, the duration of the value of the stock, one must take the first mathematical derivative of the stock value with respect to the interest rate. By putting it in the duration formula, which is the rate of change of the stock value with respect to the rate, it shows the following (whereby D presents dividend yield):

$$Duration = \frac{1}{D}.$$

The duration of a stock is therefore inversely related to its dividend yield. In other words, the higher the dividend yield, the lower the duration of the stock. In terms of the carry framework, the higher the duration of a bond or lower for a stock, the higher the bond yield (dividend yield) in relative terms to a short-term interest rate or funding rate (e.g., commercial paper in the case of companies). This also depends, however, on the shape of the yield curve. The flatter the yield curve caused by the minimal difference between long-term and short-term interest rates, the less carry return. This happens during times when the Federal Reserve hikes interest rates by a large amount. Carry in long maturity bonds is lower because that segment of the yield curve is generally flatter even when short-term interest rates are low. For stocks, carry return derived from duration does not have the same meaning as in fixed income. If a company has a high dividend yield, then its equity duration is low. Per unit of duration (dividend yield—short-term funding rate divided by equity duration), the carry per unit or risk could be high.

Relative-value Framework

Arbitrage opportunities may arise because of the mispricing of similar type securities. In U.S. Treasuries, there are bonds issued with different coupons but similar maturities, and they trade sometimes at different prices. The driving factors can vary, but in general liquidity, financing and deliverability into a bond futures contract or credit default swap are reasons why an arbitrage opportunity may exist. In stocks, such factors may be less at work because there are not identical shares issued by a group of companies in the same sector. In other words, a stock issued by company A is not identical to a stock issued by company B, even if both companies pay the same amount of dividend. This may provide in general fewer arbitrage opportunities in stocks as compared to bonds. That being said, stocks and bonds can be compared in a relative-value framework by applying some of the fixed-income relative-value techniques.

In relative value, there is a "natural" arbitrage between a cash and a futures instrument. The reason is that a cash instrument represents a spot price, while a futures price is about an expected price or a forward price. Bond futures are based on the delivery of a tangible basket of underlying bonds at some date in the future. The contracts are associated with "cash-and-carry arbitrage." The cash-and-carry strategy entails holding a long position in a bond, while simultaneously holding a short position in the bond futures contract. In a cash-and-carry trade, the long position in the underlying bond is held until the contract delivery date, and is used to cover the short futures position's obligation to deliver. In practice, an investor buys a bond that is deliverable into the futures contract, finances the bond in the repo market, and at the same time sells the bond futures contract. The bond is held until expiry of the bond futures contract, when it is delivered against the short futures position. An investor can make a gain when the cost of holding the bond is less than the gains on the futures contract.

For equities' cash-and-carry arbitrage, stock index futures can be a viable instrument. A stock index future is a cash-settled futures contract on the value of a particular stock market index. A forward price of an equity index or individual stock is calculated by computing the cost of carry of holding positions in index constituents or shares. The cost of carry is the "risk-free" interest rate because the cost of investing in stocks is the opportunity loss of earning interest on cash. The dividend yield on the index is an estimated yield because receiving dividends on the component stocks can occur at different times.

The cost-of-carry arbitrage for a stock index future would be as follows:

1) An investor buys a portfolio of shares that replicates the stock index (with proportions matching the construction of the index)
2) The portfolio is financed by secured borrowing, e.g., a stock repurchase agreement (repo)
3) The investor subsequently sells one stock index futures
4) The portfolio would be held until the last trading day of the stock futures index contract to collect and invest interim dividends received
5) On the last trading day, the underlying shares are liquidated at the moment when trading in the index future ceases and cash settles
6) The proceeds of share sale and futures settlement are used to repay the stock repo
7) The net difference between proceeds and borrowing cost would the cash-and-carry return

The main purpose of cash and carry in bond and equity futures is to estimate how fairly priced the futures contract is relative to the underlying cash instrument (e.g., individual stocks and bonds). There is a "basis" between futures and cash that presents the difference between the futures price and the (forward) prices of the underlying constituents. An investor would want to know what the fair futures price (FP) is. This price could be calculated for stock futures using the following formula:

$$FP = I0\ [1 + (r - d)].$$

The I0 is the stock index value, r is the borrowing rate, and d is the index dividend yield. This value is relatively easy to calculate. The fair futures price embeds cash and carry because of the way in which forward prices are calculated.

In bonds, commodities, and stocks, the forward price formula has similar features:

$$F = S_0 e^{(r-q)T} - \sum_{i=1}^{N} D_i e^{(r-q)(T-t_i)}.$$

The S0 is the spot price, r the "risk-free rate," q the cost of carry, and D_i the dividend paid at time t_i. By buying the stock "forward" and selling the index future or single stock future, an investor captures the basis risk. For stocks, bonds, or commodities, this is monetizing the cost of carry when such cost is low. The other way to calculate basis risk is to take the difference between the current price and the "fair price." The fair price can also be calculated as the cost of carry plus the spot price minus the forward price. Whenever the spot price is higher than the fair price, it means the cost of carry is high. Table 2.1 on page 58 shows two situations: A and B, in which the spot price is below or above the fair price. The cost of carry can be assumed as the company's cost of capital or its average interest cost when it can finance short-term in capital markets.

Table 2.1   Spot vs. forward of a hypothetical stock price

	Situation A	Situation B
spot price	100	102
cost of carry	2%	4%
Risk-free rate	4%	4%
Dividend	2%	2%
time (days)	30	30
Forward	98.36	102.24
Fair	100.037	100.038

*Fair price = Cost of Carry + (spot – forward)
*Forward = Spot stock price * e(Rf-cost of carry) + Dividend * 360/30,
whereby 360/30 is the annualized factor.

A Bond-Picking Framework

Although bonds and stocks are different in nature, there is a case to be made that there is no real difference between stock and bond picking. Security selection starts with a bottom-up analysis (credit, technicalities) and is supplemented with a top-down assessment (macroeconomic politics, corporate governance and management analysis). A micro or macro approach should see the same result: a bond or stock is fundamentally over or undervalued. The technical aspects (micro approach) that shows over- or undervaluation would be another confirmation. If that is all true, then how to pick a bond? And how would that technique help the equity investor in stock selection and asset allocation?

There are several ways in which bond picking can be applied. To start, the fixed-income universe comprises over $100 trillion in notional amount outstanding globally. There is, therefore, lots of variety in fixed-income instruments. There are ways to identify "value" when picking a bond. Bonds trade along a yield curve, and so there is a carry and roll-down return for each individual bond. Bonds with the highest carry and roll down return are called the "sweet spot" on the curve. That is the part where a bond investor can maximize carry and roll down return (although that is not without risk). The yield curve analysis is also a function of relativity because bonds trade at different yields or spreads relative to other bonds. Relative value opportunities often appear when a bond trades at a much higher yield or wider spread than a comparable bond does. There is a return in terms of yield pick-up or additional spread to LIBOR (a gauge for credit risk premium) while rolling down the yield curve.

Bonds trade with a "basis" to liquid derivatives like credit default swaps (CDS) and bond futures. There can be a profit opportunity between a bond's forward price and the futures price. This is known as the cash-and-carry arbitrage or "basis trading." The basis strategy entails buying a bond and financing it in the repo market, and subsequently delivering the bond through the futures contract. In corporate bonds, there is the Credit Default Swap (CDS) that is often used to explore opportunities between corporate cash bonds spreads and the CDS. A CDS contract is a swap that is designed to transfer the credit risk between parties. The purchaser of the swap makes payments until the final maturity of the CDS contract, whereby the payments are made to the seller of the swap. In case there is a debt default, the seller agrees to pay off the third party that defaults on the debt or loan. The CDS contract therefore functions as an insurance against default. When a CDS contract is sold, it is called "selling protection." When an investor buys a CDS contract, it is called "buying protection." An arbitrage opportunity is to buy the CDS contract and lock in the difference between the underlying bond and the CDS contract. The difference between the cash bond and CDS is called "positive" or "negative" basis. That means when a corporate bond credit risk premium (OAS spread) is wider than the CDS spread, there is a "negative basis" and when the OAS spread is tighter than CDS there is a "positive basis." When corporate bonds have a significant change in their CDS basis, there is valuation difference relative to the stock. For example, if corporate bonds of company Z trade at a significant negative basis (OAS wider than CDS), it indicates that the corporate bond has greater default risk than what the CDS contract implies. That means the corporate bond is priced with a risk that is closer to the equity of the firm. If at the same time, the stock of company Z trades with a high PE ratio or Price to Tangible book, then the negative basis of the corporate bonds suggest they are undervalued relative to the stock and CDS. The negative basis can also be compared to the put option premium of the stock. If the stock's put premiums are higher than the negative basis of the corporate bonds, that is an indication credit risk is rising and CDS protection is relatively attractive to buy (since it is lower than the OAS spread and stock put premium). By making basic comparisons between corporate bonds, CDS and stocks, the capital structure valuation can be tracked real time.

Bonds can trade special in repo financing, which may provide the opportunity to lend the security at a very favorable, low, or even negative financing rate and use the proceeds to invest in other bonds. That repo financing can be used as a form of leverage. When applied in a short period of time, the risks of excessive leverage can be mitigated. A yield curve has bonds with different coupons, and the yield curve may at times even look "kinked." That happens when interest-rate expectations shift at certain parts of the yield curve. There are mathematical functions that calculate a "spline curve." This is a theoretical yield curve that smooths yield maturities on individual bonds by treating them as zero-coupon bonds. The actual yield curve has bonds with different coupons. The difference between the actual and the spline curve is what bond fund managers and fixed-income traders use to identify "rich" or "cheap" bonds. A bond that is trading rich or cheap versus the spline curve often has something specific going on like a very high coupon, low liquidity, a special financing rate, or, for example, it is being bought back by the government.

Bonds with different maturities can be spread as a "butterfly." The butterfly is a portfolio of market value weighted, short- and long-maturity bonds compared to an intermediate maturity bond. The butterfly spread indicates whether short- and long-maturity bonds trade at a lower or higher yield historically relative to an intermediate-maturity bond. In bond market lingo, butterfly spreads identify whether the "belly" of the curve is rich or cheap versus the "wings." In a similar vein, bond investors compare bonds with short and long maturity as a yield curve spread. A yield curve trade expresses a view that a segment of the yield curve will become steeper or flatter as a result of a change in interest rate and inflation expectations. There are also statistical regression methods like principal component analysis (PCA) to analyze the yield curve. Those regressions are used to calculate three effects: the level, the slope, and the curvature of the yield curve. The method shows that bonds with high convexity (that measures the change in duration) can be at times under- or overvalued to bonds with lower convexity. There are bonds that are "on the run," which have been recently issued and are considered to be benchmark bonds. There are bonds that are "off the run," which are no longer issued but which have maintained a benchmark status. That means these bonds remain tradable in the secondary market. There is a spread between on-the-run and off-the-run bonds that is a measure of liquidity. In times of distress, the spread between on-the-run and off-the-run bonds can become significantly wider. That is a sign secondary market liquidity has materially deteriorated.

There is a technique that is called "coupon stacking." In mortgage-backed securities (MBS), the coupon stack is often traded when interest rates rise or fall. In general, bonds in a certain segment of the curve can be stacked by coupon in order to obtain higher accruing interest paid. This strategy is for investors who seek coupon return instead of price return. The same strategy is applied in laddering that aims at maximizing coupon return.

Liquidity in the bond market can be measured by inventories. The secondary market in bonds is almost entirely driven by what is available in dealer inventories. Those positions are either proprietary positions or leftover positions from a recent new issue, or securities bought from customers. The bond market over the years has transformed significantly, with many corporate bonds traded on electronic platforms. The bids or offerings in those bonds, however, come almost exclusively from inventory. To that end, the repo market allows dealers and market makers to take a short positioning in bonds. The repo market has been shrinking since 2009 because of the Dodd-Frank Act and other regulations. As a result of inventory not being equally dispersed among dealers, there can be significant price discrepancies in certain bonds. Understanding the depth of the secondary market by understanding positioning and "color" (a term for information) about who is trading what bonds can make a meaningful difference in achieving excess returns.

Fund managers, dealers, and traders often switch bonds. There are several reasons for switching. A switch is meant to improve in yield, to pick up in spread, and to address credit quality. A reason to switch can be to bolster liquidity or to benefit from currency changes. Other factors that drive bond switching can be to average high dollar prices. That means by blending low and higher dollar price bonds, the liquidity of the portfolio can be improved. A bond switch can also be done to lengthen or shorten the duration risk of the portfolio. Active bond switching can add alpha to a portfolio, but not without potentially significant transaction costs. Switching bonds can also be viewed in the context of bond index arbitrage. Bond indices are a representative of the fixed-income universe. When bonds are bought that are not in the index but are permissioned to be acquired, such bonds add alpha and tracking error to the portfolio. Tracking error is the difference between the portfolio return and the index return as an expression of the portfolio's volatility (measured by standard deviation). When an investor actively trades bonds that are not in the index, such a strategy is called "off index bets." The investor can pick specific bonds that are not in the index even when the respective issuer is part of the index universe.

Another way of enhancing the yield on a bond investment is by "selling noise." Whenever there is lots of noise that is treated the same as information, options with a longer maturity get overpriced. That is because when short-term volatility is used as input to value options with a longer expiration, there is a maturity mismatch. This often happens with callable or putable corporate bonds or in some cases municipal bonds. Those bonds see their OAS spreads widen quickly when short-term volatility picks up. The spread widening may not be justified by fundamentals, and therefore there is at times opportunity to "sell the noise" by buying callable longer maturity bonds. Bond futures and high-yield debt have embedded options that can get overpriced when short-term volatility is high. The mispricing of (embedded) options provides an opportunity to add additional return to the portfolio collected from option premiums. Those premiums should normalize after events such as political crises or a military conflict subsides.

There are also ways to identify arbitrage boundaries in fixed income. An arbitrage boundary is a situation in which there is a specific range or time when arbitrage is profitable. This boundary can be seen in liquid, short-term futures markets like Eurodollar futures. These futures are traded on the Chicago Mercantile Exchange. They provide a market in which an investor can borrow or lend short-term funds up to a specified date in the future. Eurodollar futures are based on the underlying LIBOR index. A bank could arbitrage borrowing and lending in money markets by borrowing short, selling Eurodollar futures, and then lending out the funds to a date further out in the future. These are called "two-way transactions," and they should net out cash flows when Eurodollar futures are fairly priced. If Eurodollar futures are not fairly priced, then a riskless profit could be earned. The two-way transactions present, therefore, "arbitrage boundaries." When an investor buys a longer maturity corporate or Treasury bond, financing the bond in the repo market or borrow on margin, and selling a Eurodollar futures, there is spread to be earned. That spread is a "riskless" profit when Eurodollar futures are "mispriced" because of excessive interest-rate expectations. Mispricing of a futures contract relative to a cash instrument produces the same profit opportunity whether that is a stock or a bond.

Let us Put the Frameworks to Work

The preceding analysis discussed a variety of fixed-income strategies and relative-value methods. It is important to understand that not every carry, relative-value, or bond-picking method is directly applicable to stocks. That is because bonds and stocks are not mathematically the same instrument even though they both present a discounted stream of cash flow. An important component of bond investment strategy is the yield curve. In stocks, a yield curve is a theoretical concept and is not practical. Even though dividend stocks have duration, and stocks in general have a forward price, the yield curve strategy is better applied in bonds than in stocks. Stocks can be financed on margin and that cost of financing can be measured relative to their yield derived from free cash flow or earnings. The same comparison can be made relative to the dividend yield or return on invested capital. A stock investor can earn carry when comparing finance cost with the yields from free cash flow, earnings, dividend, or invested capital. A stock investor can also do a "basis trade" between individual stocks and stock index futures. In addition, in a stock portfolio, much like a bond portfolio, an investor can buy stocks of companies not included in a broader index. Just like in fixed income, there are opportunities to sell noise when short-term stock volatility is high. Last, a stock investor can design an equity ladder by stacking stable dividend stocks. When it comes to a stock or bond portfolio strategy in general, the most important part of the analysis is the fundamentals. When stocks and bonds are compared on a fundamental basis, an investor has to take a view on the capital structure of a company. That requires a thorough understanding of the specifics of the company's outstanding debt and covenants, as well as the specific rights of the stock holder.

The capital structure is the assembly of the investable universe the company plans to use to make capital expenditure decisions, mergers, or acquisitions, to pay dividends, or to

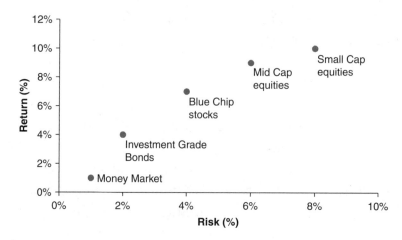

Figure 2.1   Asset allocation frontier along the capital structure.
Source: Author, historical averages for risk and return estimated by Shiller/Ibbotson.

buy back stock. Fundamental analysis ties back to asset allocation, in which bonds and stocks play a pivotal role in sizing
the appropriate weights within a portfolio. Stock and bond
returns present a frontier, as shown in Figure 2.1. The bond-
picking frameworks discussed can help in allocating along
the frontier that presents the capital structure of a company.

For practical purposes, the analysis focuses on major sectors of the S&P 500 index. Those sectors represent stocks
from companies that issue stock and debt and that are from
different industries and have multinational operations. *It is
important to note that the author has no position in the companies at the time of writing this book. The analysis is not intended
and should not be viewed as investment advice to sell or purchase the shares of the specific companies discussed.*

Utilities

Utility stocks have long been thought of as stocks that
behave like bonds. That is because of their stable revenue
model and historically anchored dividend payout ratios.

Utility stocks exhibit fixed-income characteristics in terms of stable cash flow streams. They may therefore be a sector in which some of the previously discussed fixed-income frameworks can be applied. There is an easy comparison to make between S&P 500 utilities stocks. Table 2.2 on page 69 shows the S&P 500 Utility sector. There are general stock valuation measures posted, such as the PE ratio, price-to-sales (PS) ratio, ROE, and cash dividend coverage. Analysis of Table 2.2 would suggest that on a comparison basis, Pacific Gas and Electric (PG&E) is not an attractive stock. Although it has a high PE multiple, its earnings growth is negative and there is low cash dividend coverage. On top of that, the company has a low ROE with sluggish sales growth and a high debt-to-equity ratio. This basic comparison would suggest that PG&E is a "rich" stock. Public Service Enterprise (PSE) stock, in contrast, may look "cheap." It has the lowest PE multiple in the sector, a high earnings growth and ROE, and its enterprise to earnings before interest and taxes (EV/EBITDA) multiple suggests there could more upside potential. A stock picker reading this table would add more factors to the analysis to ensure the valuation of the stock accounts for all aspects. That additional analysis may argue the opposite conclusion. For example, in 2014 some analysts noted that the cash contribution of deferred taxes might significantly reduce the need for PG&E to raise equity. The lower share count was expected to increase the earnings power of the company, making PG&E attractive on a valuation basis. PSE, however, had been hurt in prior years by higher expenses to repair facilities and restore electricity to customers in the wake of "Superstorm Sandy" and other storm-related expenses. Its 2014 second-quarter earnings fell 36 percent as the power company's operating revenue declined, which was driven by higher operating expenses. This gives a different comparison picture of the rich/cheap analysis. In other words, there are many reasons why or why not a stock is under- or overvalued.

What if there were a different way of analyzing these stocks? If PG&E is a rich stock on multiples, but because it has the potential to appreciate in price, could the fixed-income frameworks provide additional insight? Utility stocks have relatively stable dividend yields, free cash flow yields, and return on invested capital. Although the debt-to-equity ratios shown in Table 2.2 is mostly over 100, the debt profiles of utility companies seem relatively spread out, with limited rollover risk of short-term debt. When we look at utility stocks, "carry" is probably the most logical fixed-income type of return that may provide another conclusion to the fundamental stock valuation. Other fixed-income analysis included could be forward price comparison to the cash price, the laddering or stapling of dividend yields, evaluation of stock duration, and the basis between futures and cash stock prices. Based on each of the stocks' fixed-income valuation measures, Table 2.3 on page 70 shows the following comparison.

Table 2.3 would also suggest that PG&E is not an attractive stock on a carry basis. It has a significant negative free cash flow yield, and the simple carry measures of dividend yield and free cash flow versus cost of debt show little or negative carry for the stock. PSE, however, has a better profile, albeit not the best in terms of carry from free cash flow and dividend return. The better carry stock appears to be Duke Energy, which has positive carry overall due to high dividend and lowest weighted average cost of capital. Fundamental equity analysts would argue in the case of Duke that there is a convergence of positive investment measures that are drivers for growth in earnings per share, increase in net income, and revenue growth. These

Table 2.2 S&P 500 Utility stocks comparison

	Price/ EPS	Price/ Sales	Price/ Cashflow	EV/ EBITDA	EPS Growth	Sales Growth	ROE	Tot Debt/ Equity	Cash Div Coverage
Duke	15.74	2.08	8.59	12.33	16.07	4.96	5.45	104.06	1.32
Dominion	20.48	3.17	13.41	14.85	106.54	-0.16	13.63	211.1	N.A.
Southern	15.51	2.2	6.37	9.32	7.18	6.87	11.89	126.24	1.23
AE	14.8	1.58	5.37	8.57	16.07	9.65	10.77	118.25	1.77
PG&E	30.04	1.37	6.71	10.11	-23.81	4.84	5.13	102.6	0.89
Xcel	17.08	1.42	6.36	9.63	-5.18	7.55	10.11	126.38	1.67
Nextra	23.35	2.68	7.98	11.65	11.21	9.75	11.12	162.52	1.63
Sempra	25.86	2.45	15.35	13.43	-15.64	2.42	9.99	122.89	1.73
PSE	13.09	1.82	5.77	7.69	10.35	4.44	10.36	76.22	1.61

Source: FRB, SEC, September 2014.

Table 2.3 Utility sector different measures of "yield"

	Cost of Debt	WACC	ROIC	Dividend Yield	Free cash flow yield	"carry" vs. Free Cash Flow	"carry" vs. Dividend
Duke Energy	2.45%	4.60%	5.20%	4.25%	3.8%	1.4%	1.80%
Dominion Resources	2.50%	5.60%	9.10%	3.37%	-1.8%	-4.3%	0.87%
Southern Co	2.46%	5.30%	6.92%	4.81%	1.8%	-0.7%	2.35%
American Electric	1.90%	5.60%	6.79%	3.75%	1.30%	-0.6%	1.85%
PG&E Corp	2.70%	5.40%	4.99%	3.97%	-9.80%	-12.5%	1.27%
Xcel Energy Inc	2.10%	5.50%	6.43%	3.85%	-6%	-8.1%	1.75%
NextEra Energy Inc	2.10%	5.70%	6.13%	3.05%	4.98%	2.9%	0.95%
Sempra Energy	2.50%	5.80%	6.74%	2.49%	-3.60%	-6.1%	-0.01%
Public Service Enterprise	2%	5.60%	6.33%	3.86%	2.14%	0.1%	1.86%

Source: Yahoo finance, FRB, SEC September 2014. Carry vs. Free cash flow = Free cash flow yield – cost of debt. Carry vs. Dividend = Dividend yield – cost of debt. WACC = weighted average cost of Capital, ROIC = Return on Invested Capital.

strengths could outweigh the fact that the company has a weak operating cash flow. The analysis in Tables 2.2 and 2.3 can be combined to judge whether a stock is really "rich, cheap, or fair." To take that analysis a step further, Table 2.4 displays each stock's forward and fair price, net earnings yields, CDS, equity duration, and beta to the S&P 500.

At first glance, Table 2.4 suggests that Duke, PSE, and Southern Company are attractive on the basis of their stock prices, which trade below fair value, and they have a lower stock duration as well as high net earnings yields. On that comparison, Duke and Southern Company stocks look "cheap," while PG&E stock looks "rich." In a fixed-income analogy, when we analyze Table 2.4, there is a way to express "carry per unit of duration." In bonds, often the excess return per unit of risk is a useful measure for determining the suitability of the bond investment. The longer the maturity of a bond, the less carry per unit of duration can be earned, even if the yield curve is upward sloping. As argued previously,

Table 2.4 Utility sector and different measures of price and duration

	Current price	Forward price	Fair price	CDS (basispoints)	Beta to S&P 500	Stock duration	Net Earnings yield
Duke	74.38	74.48	74.403	20.5	0.79	23.5	6.3%
Dominion	68.9	68.96	68.925	37.5	0.76	29.7	4.9%
Southern	43.69	44.03	43.71	N/A	0.67	20.8	6.4%
AE	53.28	53.15	53.3	24.5	0.81	26.7	6.7%
PG&E	45.84	42.64	45.81	52	0.67	25.2	3.3%
Xcel	31.29	31.47	31.309	32	0.77	26.0	5.8%
Nextra	95.14	94.65	95.65	75	0.78	32.8	4.3%
Sempra	106	105.85	106.019	35.5	0.73	40.2	3.8%
PSE	38.3	38.1	38.321	99.41	0.67	25.9	7.6%

Source: Yahoo Finance, FRB, SEC. September 2014.

*Fair price = Cost of Carry + (spot –forward), *Forward = Spot stock price *e(Rf-cost of carry) + Dividend. Rf *360/30, Stock duration 1/Dividend yield, Net earnings yield = 1/PE – total cost of debt.

stocks do not have a yield curve, and although Table 2.4 shows that for each stock's duration there is an earnings yield, the so-called equity yield curve is inverted. The higher the earnings yield, free cash flow yield, or dividend yield, the lower the stock duration. In fixed income, this is typically the opposite. The higher the yield, the longer the maturity of the bond and thereby its duration (except during certain times when short-term interest rates rise significantly due to very tight monetary policy or default risks). The most effective way to calculate stock carry per unit of stock duration is to take the difference of the stock's forward and current price and divide that by the stock's duration. Table 2.5 shows the comparison.

Carry/Duration = (Stock Forward Price – Stock Spot
Price) * 100/Stock Duration. Stock
duration 1/dividend yield

This ratio includes the dividend yield in the stock's forward price and the excess return (carry) earned expressed in unit of equity duration. Table 2.5 once more re-enforces that PG&E is an unattractive stock as it earns significant

Table 2.5   Stock carry per unit of duration

	Carry/duration
Duke Energy	0.425
Dominion Resources	0.2022
Southern Co	1.6354
American Electric	−0.4875
PG&E Corp	−12.704
Xcel Energy Inc	0.693
NextEra Energy Inc	−1.4945
Sempra Energy	−0.3735
Public Service Enterprise	−0.772

Source: Yahoo Finance, FRB, SEC. September 2014.

negative carry over the life of the equity (free) cash flow. Southern Company stands out best as the carry multiple suggests that investors will be 1.6x rewarded in earning dividend per unit of equity risk. In principle the concept of a stock total return when applying fixed-income analysis would the same as the coupon (e.g. dividend) plus capital gains. This "total return" is driven by carry, the excess return earned by the equity holder after stripping out the weight average cost of capital (e.g., debt). This carry framework can be applied to any stock cost of or equity index as long the shares pay a stable dividend. If the dividend stream is irregular or uncertain, the carry framework does *not* work. Hence, the more stable the dividend, the more convincing the argument that a stock behaves likes a bond. The measure of stock carry per unit of equity duration is therefore perhaps the most effective way of identifying stocks with fixed-income features. This has to be underscored, however, by the stability of the equity carry multiple (equity carry per unit of equity duration). The more stable carry per unit of equity duration, the higher the excess return from free cash flow when compared to the overall cost of capital.

In Table 2.6 on page 74 the carry framework is applied to the S&P 500 Index and its individual index constituents. By calculating the cost of carry (weighted average cost of capital for each index) and assuming a "risk-free" rate of 2 percent, each index has a forward price. The equity carry per unit of equity index duration can be seen on the left side of the column. Utility stocks may be viable for a "ladder" strategy because their dividend payout ratio has been historically stable. If we take a sample of the utility companies shown in Table 2.7 on page 75 the dividend pay dates are somewhat spread out. The most important assumption would be that the dividend stays stable and has

Table 2.6 Equity carry/unit of equity duration across sectors of the S&P 500

Sector	Dividend Yield (%)	WACC (%)	Carry duration (yrs)	Spot price	Forward Price	Carry/unit of equity duration (bps)
S&P 500 INDEX	2.0	6.0	51	1950	1952	394
S&P 500 TELECOM SERV IDX	4.7	4.5	21	638	639	439
S&P 500 UTILITIES INDEX	4.0	5.0	25	633	634	542
S&P 500 CONS STAPLES IDX	2.8	5.5	35	562	563	181
S&P 500 MATERIALS INDEX	23	5.0	43	519	521	433
S&P 500 ENERGY INDEX	2.1	5.5	47	442	442.5	196
S&P 500 INDUSTRIALS IDX	1.9	5.2	52	435	436	212
S&P 500 FINANCIALS INDEX	1.7	4.8	60	289	291	344
S&P 500 HEALTH CARE IDX	1.7	4.6	61	279	281	351

Source: FRB, SEC. Carry/Duration = (Stock Forward Price– Stock Spot Price) *100/Stock Duration. Forward = Spot stock price *e(Rf-cost of carry) + Dividend. Rf * 360/360.

Table 2.7 Utility sector dividend yields and payment dates

	Dividend Yield	Payout Frequency	Ex-date	Pay date	Div growth 5yr	Dividend amount
Duke Energy	4.25%	quarterly	11/12/2014	12/16/2014	2.25%	$ 0.75
Dominion Resources	3.37%	quarterly	11/25/2014	11/28/2014	6.50%	$ 0.58
Southern Co	4.81%	quarterly	10/30/2014	12/6/2014	3.75%	$ 0.52
American Electric	3.75%	quarterly	11/6/2014	12/10/2014	4.36%	$ 0.50
PG&E Corp	3.97%	quarterly	11/8/2014	10/15/2014	1.98%	$ 0.45
Xcel Energy Inc	3.85%	quarterly	11/12/2014	12/16/2014	3.85%	$ (0.06)
NextEra Energy Inc	3.05%	quarterly	11/25/2014	11/28/2014	3.05%	$ 0.05
Sempra Energy	2.49%	quarterly	10/30/2014	12/6/2014	2.49%	$ (0.04)
Public Service Enterprise	3.86%	quarterly	11/6/2014	12/10/2014	3.86%	$ 0.02

Source: FRB, SEC, November 2014.

a positive growth rate. An investor could stack up the stocks in table 2.7 and use the dividend proceeds either to reinvest in a higher paying dividend stock or for cash flow to make other payments.

The stock ladder would be focused on the different dates that involve dividend payments. The declaration date is the date on which a company announces the specific dividend payment along with the holder of record date (aka record date) and the payment date. For example, in Table 2.7 Duke announces that a dividend payment of 75 cents per share will be payable, December 16, 2014 (the payment date) to all shareholders of record at the close of business on November 2, 2014 (holder of record date). The ex-dividend date (typically two trading days before the holder of record date for US securities) is the day on which a company begins trading without the dividend. In order to have a claim on a dividend, shares must be purchased no later than the last business day before the ex-dividend date. A company trading ex-dividend will have the upcoming dividend subtracted from the share price at the start of the trading day. Many times, the price of a stock will increase in anticipation of the upcoming dividend as the ex-dividend date approaches, yet may fall back by the amount of the dividend on the ex-dividend date. An investor in a stock ladder in the traditional sense of fixed income would be interested in capturing a stable dividend that could be reinvested or used as cash flow. Although the strict ladder definition of stacking bond maturities to diversify duration risk does not apply to stocks, the coupon (dividend) stacking does. Investors would seek a sector with stable dividend payout ratios to express a ladder strategy. The dividend ladder could also be combined with a bond ladder. For example, an investor could purchase several utility stocks and the bonds issued by those companies. There is considerable credit risk involved in that combination. A perhaps better way to construct a portfolio of a dividend and coupon ladder would be to diversify between stable dividend-paying stocks, low-duration high coupon-paying Treasury bonds, and short maturity municipal bonds with stable ratings.

Multicurrency

A currency is a two-sided relationship. It is a ratio that expresses a home currency in a unit of foreign currency. In global fixed-income portfolios, the currency is a return enhancement on top of holding a bond denominated in a foreign currency. The coupon earned on a German bond plus the gain from the Euro currency presents (all else being equal) the total return. A similar idea of earning dividend and currency gains exists for stocks. A German company that pays regular dividend would provide the international equity investor a dividend plus (potential) currency return and stock price gains (or losses). As mentioned earlier, stocks of multinational companies can be issued in different currencies. An investor can take an opportunity to purchase a stock of a US multinational currency that is also denominated in Euro. In other words, there is a "cross-currency" aspect to internationally listed shares. A way to benefit from the currency return (called the "carry component of currency") is by using forward contracts or cross-currency basis swaps. These instruments are not always available for individual investors. There are, however, many funds, exchange-traded funds (ETFs) and closed-end funds that offer an explicit strategy that aims at capturing the carry return from currencies. There are also brokerage houses that offer their clients accounts that can invest in foreign currency.

For the present analysis, the stocks of several large multinational companies are taken as an example to demonstrate how international fixed income can be applied to determine equity valuation. There are many companies listed on the S&P 500, NASDAQ, and Dow Jones that operate like a multinational. They do so because their products have a worldwide audience and demand. There are others that argue multinationals are driven by "tax inversion." They have entangled internationally located branches that allow these companies to drive down their weighted average corporate tax rate in order to maximize earnings per share. Multinationals also exist because of cross-border opportunities, mergers and acquisitions, and demand from investors, who seek currency return per share. About 40 percent of the S&P 500 Index has companies that are listed as multinationals. This explains why the US stock market as a whole may no longer solely represent US GDP. The S&P 500, Dow Jones, and NASDAQ have continued to outgrow the US economy since 2007. Their combined earnings power is decoupled from US GDP. As the global economy healed following the financial crisis, these three indices have relentlessly resumed their upward momentum despite intermittent slowdowns in the US and European economies. As part of these indices, the group of multinationals used in the analysis are Ford, General Electric (GE), ExxonMobil, IBM, McDonald's, and Amazon.

Ford is a $129 billion revenue company, with 51 percent of its profits from overseas. Foreign automakers sell a lot of cars in the United States, but US carmakers are global, too. Ford, like General Motors, has a strong presence in Canada and Europe, while General Motors (GM), through a joint venture, is one of the biggest carmakers in China—where its profits sometimes exceed those earned in the United States.

Ford, meanwhile, has emerged as the strongest domestic automaker, which helped overseas sales. GE has $149 billion in revenue, 54 percent from overseas. GE prides itself on its international footprint, although a few industrial firms, such as Caterpillar and 3M, earn an even larger portion of their revenue overseas. GE has sizable operations in Europe, China, Russia, and India, along with a significant presence in Africa, the Middle East, and other parts of the developing world. Overseas operations include infrastructure development and investment activities led by GE's financial arm. IBM has a total of $100 billion in revenue, of which 64 percent is gained internationally. Like GE, IBM is another old-line firm that has grown roots throughout the globe and profited handsomely from globalization. IBM piggybacks on the global growth of its many corporate clients, while also pursuing new initiatives such as a big wireless-phone network in Africa. IBM aims to draw nearly 30 percent of its revenue from emerging markets by 2015. ExxonMobil trumps $342 billion in revenue, and 45 percent comes from overseas sales. Like other big oil companies, Exxon goes where the oil is and sells to customers throughout the globe. Exxon derives slightly more revenue from overseas operations than rivals like Chevron or ConocoPhillips. With $24 billion in revenue, McDonald's depends mostly on foreign markets; 66 percent of its revenues come from overseas. McDonald's earns the majority of its revenue from Europe and Asia. McDonald's experience taught it that it cannot necessarily sell the same burgers and fries in foreign markets, which is why its global operations focus on making sure foreign outlets fit into the local culture. At about 400 stores in China, McDonald's even delivers its products. Last, Amazon has $34 billion in revenue, and 45 percent of that is from overseas (online) activities. A lot of dot-com businesses take their time expanding overseas, since growth in the digital sector here in the United States is usually brisk enough to keep them busy. But Amazon has been around long enough to have set up robust operations in Canada, several European countries, Japan, and even China.

Ford, General Electric, ExxonMobil, IBM, McDonald's, and Amazon shares have dual listings. Most of them are listed in Europe, Asia, and Canada. Therefore, buying any of these stocks provides opportunity directly or indirectly to benefit from currency returns. The reason is because companies hedge themselves against the currency risk from their international operations. The total revenue in dollars therefore consists of different foreign currency streams. In a way, the return of these stocks listed on a respective US stock exchange embeds foreign currency return from overseas branches. A fundamental analyst would strip out the different parts of revenue generated in each foreign location and express them as earnings per local listed share. A partial picture that emerges is that in some parts of the world, the foreign EPS can be higher than the domestic EPS, albeit they all sum up into the company's total earnings. However, for investors there is an interesting opportunity. The stock listed on a foreign exchange may trade at a premium to the stock listed on the domestic exchange. That premium largely consists out of currency gain. Table 2.8 on page 81 shows for each stock the share price in both domestic and foreign countries. There is an implied currency return that is calculated for each stock. An investor could use this measure to compare multinationals.

The "implied exchange rate" is the ratio of the domestic share price to the foreign share price. The excess currency return is the implied exchange rate divided by the actual

Table 2.8   Domestic and foreign stock price and the implied exchange rate

Company	US stock price	EUR stock price	Implied exchange rate	vs. actual exchange rate
Ford	14.59	11.605	1.2572	0.5%
IBM	188.67	148.77	1.2682	1.4%
GE	25.4	20.1	1.2637	1.0%
McDonald's	94.86	75.76	1.2521	0.1%
ExxonMobil	93.92	75.15	1.2498	−0.1%
Amazon	322.74	259.73	1.2426	−0.7%

Source: FRB, SEC. October 2014. The US stock price is the shares listed in the United States and the EUR stock price is the shares listed in Europe. Their ratio expresses the implied exchange rate. EUR exchange rate early October was 1.2510. The implied/actual exchange rate is the excess currency return premium/discount implied by the foreign share price. In case of, for example GE, this is 188.67/148.77 = 1.2682. Then 1.2682/1.2510 = 1% currency premium.

exchange rate. It may not come as a surprise that IBM and GE have the highest share of their revenue coming from foreign markets (64 percent and 54 percent respectively) from the shares listed in Table 2.8.

Another way of looking at currency returns, is to analyze shares hedged in a foreign currency. For example the shares in Table 2.8 that are denominated in Euro, are hedged back to US dollars. This hedging is a method often used in global fixed income. The yield of, for example, a German bond denominated in Euro would be expressed in a yield denominated in dollars. This is a function of the interest-rate differential between Germany and the United States that is expressed by the foreign exchange (FX) swap agreement. The other component is called a "currency basis swap." An FX swap agreement is a contract in which one party borrows one currency from, and simultaneously lends another to, the second party. Each party uses the repayment obligation to its counterparty as collateral, and the amount of repayment is fixed at the FX forward rate as of the start of the contract.

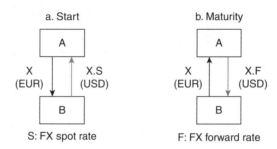

Figure 2.2   FX swap agreement.
Source: Bank of International Settlements www.bis.org.

Thus, FX swaps can be viewed as FX "risk-free" collateralized borrowing/lending. Figure 2.2 illustrates the fund flows involved in a Euro/US dollar swap as an example. At the start of the contract, A borrows X·S USD from, and lends X EUR to, B, where S is the FX spot rate. When the contract expires, A returns X·F USD to B and B returns X EUR to A, where F is the FX forward rate as of the start.

FX swaps have been employed to hedge foreign currencies, both for financial institutions and their customers, including exporters and importers, as well as institutional investors who wish to hedge their positions. They are also frequently used for speculative trading, typically by combining two offsetting positions with different original maturities. FX swaps are most liquid at terms shorter than one year, but transactions with longer maturities have been increasing in recent years.

A cross-currency basis swap agreement is a contract in which one party borrows one currency from another party and simultaneously lends the same value, at current spot rates, of a second currency to that party. The parties involved in basis swaps are generally financial institutions, either acting on their own or as agents for nonfinancial corporations. Figure 2.3 on page 83 illustrates the flow of

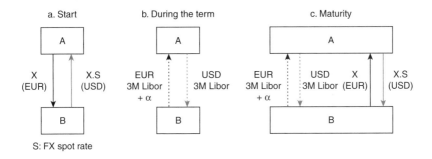

Figure 2.3   Cross-currency basis swap.

Source: Bank of International Settlements, www.bis.org.

funds involved in a Euro/US dollar swap. At the start of the contract, A borrows X·S USD from B, and lends X EUR to, B. During the contract term, A receives EUR 3M Libor + α from B, and pays USD 3M Libor to B every three months. The term α represents the price of the basis swap, agreed upon by the counterparties at the start of the contract. When the contract expires, A returns X·S USD to B, and B returns X EUR to A. The term S is the spot exchange rate, which is the same FX spot rate at the start of the contract. Although the structure of cross-currency basis swaps differs from FX swaps, the former basically serve the same economic purpose as the latter, except for the exchange of floating rates during the contract term. Cross-currency basis swaps have been employed to fund foreign currency investments, both by financial institutions and their customers, including multinational corporations engaged in foreign direct investment. They have also been used as a tool for converting liabilities, particularly by issuers of bonds denominated in foreign currencies. Mirroring the tenor of the transactions they are meant to fund, most cross-currency basis swaps are long term, generally ranging between one year and thirty years maturity.

Table 2.9   Hedged dividend yield

	US div yield	EU Div yield	Interest dif.	Basis swap	EU div yield hedge to US
Ford	3.44	3.21	−1.1	−0.16	4.47
IBM	2.33	2.20	−1.3	−0.16	3.66
GE	3.49	3.39	−1.3	−0.16	4.85
Mc Donald's	3.72	3.62	−0.7	−0.16	4.48
Exxon-Mobile	2.92	2.76	−1	−0.16	3.92

Source: SEC, FRB, October 2014. Dividend yields are in gross terms. Interest-rate difference is defined as the difference between the yield on a five-year maturity USD- and Euro-denominated corporate bond for each of the respective companies. The Euro dollar basis swap also has a five-year maturity. Of note is that Amazon has not paid a dividend. The EUR dividend yield hedged to USD, for example, GE is calculated as 3.39% − (−1.3% + −0.16) = 4.85%.

To take the example of the stocks shown in Table 2.9, their hedged dividend yields to dollars is somewhat of an odd concept. A dividend yield is not the same as a coupon because it is less stable and not fixed. Expressing dividend yield in foreign currency terms would provide a different indication of what the currency premium is really worth. For an equity investor to precisely follow the fixed-income strategy of FX hedged yields, one would have to look at the dividend yield in foreign stock market versus the domestic stock market (which may not always be so clear). The investor should also incorporate the interest-rate difference of debt issued in foreign markets and that of debt issued in the local market. Unlike with bonds, the hedged dividend yield has perpetual duration. The FX forward contract is bound by a maximum maturity, that is, typically no longer than ten years. Despite the caveats, a comparison of hedged dividend yields may provide some insight into a stock's attractiveness. In Table 2.9, the six stocks are listed again in terms of their dividend yield and hedged dividend yield.

FX forwards and basis swaps are not always observable in the financial media. The best way to analyze the interest-rate differential is by comparing where each company funds its debt in different currencies. In the case of GE, its five-year maturity corporate bond, the GE 2.3% 1/2019 bond denominated in US dollars, yields 1.91 percent. The GE Euro-denominated corporate bond, GE 6% 1/2019, yields 0.62 percent. The interest difference of 1.3 percent between the bonds reflects an approximate interest difference between US and Europe. In October 2014, the difference between 5-year US and Euro government bond yields was also around 1.4 percent. Thus, calculating a hedged dividend yield on stocks does not necessarily require an understanding of the complexity of FX forwards and basis swaps. Table 2.9 presents a comparison in which dividend yields in Euros are expressed in terms of the US dollar. GE stands out in terms of its Euro dividend hedged to dollar at 4.85 percent. This is not surprising because the company has the highest share of its revenues earned offshore. As shown in Table 2.9, GE seems to have value in terms of currency premium reflected in its hedged dividend yield as well as stock price difference between its domestic and foreign listed shares. The analysis suggests that when analyzing multinational companies, taking a fixed-income approach may provide additional insight into relative valuation. The foreign currency premium is a relative-value measure, as compared to a fundamental measure like price per earnings (PE), earnings per share (EPS), price to book (PB) and so forth.

Bond Switches and Pairs Trading

A common technique in fixed income is switching between bonds. Net of transaction fees, a bond switch, may enhance the yield of the bond investment. The yield gets enhanced by, for example, switching from a short maturity and lower yielding bond, to a longer maturity and higher yielding bond. The switch may produce a higher price return in a falling rate environment. That is because when switching from short to longer maturity, the duration of the bond investment extends. A longer duration in a falling interest rate environment allows for higher price increases than in the case of a short maturity bond. When interest rates rise, a "coupon switch" may be preferred to cushion against price loss. The reason for that is a higher coupon somewhat reduces the duration of a bond and hence to a degree can limit bond price decline when rates go up. Fixed-income investors often ride the yield curve by switching from short- to longer maturity bonds when the curve is upward sloping. When there is curve inversion (yields on short maturity bonds are higher than long maturity bonds), it may be beneficial to switch from long- to short-maturity bonds if inflation is stable or falling, and there is no default risk. Arbitrage traders may switch bonds with similar coupons and nearby maturities to capture tiny price or yield differences. Bond switching also entails a change in credit risk exposure. When an investor exchanges bonds with different credit ratings, a higher return may be achieved by improvement in the credit rating or alternatively a higher yield may be obtained by taking more risk in lower-rated securities. Returns in fixed income are therefore often derived from switching bonds. These frequent adjustments are part of an overall bond picking strategy. In stocks, switching of shares between different companies is not all too different from switching bonds. In equities, there is a strategy called "pairs trading." That strategy is selling one stock and buying another to capture or pay a predefined price spread. Execution of this type of trade when dealing with many small executions may help reduce slippage in transaction costs.

This trading strategy is used when an investor wishes to add alpha to a portfolio without changing credit exposure. This usually occurs when a company has two outstanding stocks with different voting rights. The trading strategy can also be applied in merger situations, or when two stocks are highly correlated because the companies operate in the same industry. The "pair trade" is a market-neutral trading strategy enabling traders to profit from virtually any market conditions: uptrend, downtrend, or sideways movement. This strategy is categorized as a statistical arbitrage or convergence trading strategy. The strategy monitors performance of two historically correlated securities. When the correlation between the two securities temporarily weakens, that is, one stock moves up while the other moves down, the pairs trade would be to short the outperforming stock and to go long the underperforming stock, betting that the "spread" between the two will eventually converge. The divergence within a pair can be caused by temporary supply/demand changes, large buy/ sell orders for one security, the reaction to important news about one of the companies, and so on.

To be successful in pairs strategies, the investor needs to be able to size positioning, time markets, and make quick decisions. In stocks pairs trading, like in bond switches, the profitable opportunities are scarce. A stock pair or bond pair that seems misaligned in price difference is likely to be arbitraged quickly. In stocks there are pairs like Coca Cola and Pepsi, Facebook and Twitter, Ford and GM, JPMorgan Chase and Bank of America, United Airlines and American Airlines, and so forth. The price spread between these stocks shows a discount or premium that is a rating difference and company structure difference. The price spreads are related to the difference in CDS, OAS, and bond price spreads. For example, there is a relationship between Coca Cola and

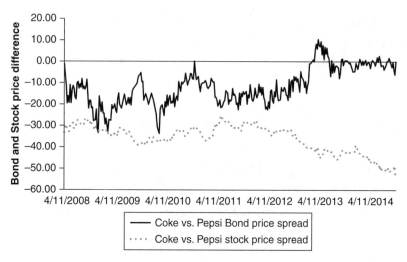

Figure 2.4   Coke vs. Pepsi stock and bond price spread.
Source: SEC, NYFRB, weekly data 2008–2014.

Pepsi stock price spread and bond price differential, as shown in Figure 2.4.

At first glance, the figure shows that the Coke bonds are higher in price than the Pepsi bonds. By the same token, the Coke stock price is lower than the Pepsi stock price. Does that mean Coke bonds are relatively "cheap" to Pepsi bonds and that Coke stock price is relatively "rich" to Pepsi stock? Pepsi and Coke have similar activities, but a different capital structure. For instance, Coke relies more on short-term debt than Pepsi does by approximately a difference of 15 percent to 20 percent, according to its latest earnings filings. In other words, Coke has a higher short-term debt "rollover risk" that may be reflected in its stock price because such risk may increase the probability of bankruptcy. However, Coke's long-term debt has a favorable rating (A-), and Coke's senior unsecured CDS spread is lower (25 basis points) than that of Pepsi (37 basis points). It is known that Coke and Pepsi have been in a "cola war" since the 1980s. Notably, Coke and Pepsi have very few differences in multiples. PE, Price to Book, and EV/EBDITA are fairly close, and their total stock price returns since the lows of March 2009 are also in proximity (92% vs. 99%). There is a capital structure opportunity by switching from Coke bonds to Pepsi bonds, while moving from Pepsi stock to Coke stock.

When we think of pairs trading or bond switching, the term "arbitrage" comes to mind. Arbitrage exists when there is a profit opportunity between two securities as a result of a price discrepancy. For arbitrage to hold, the two securities can trade in the same market or separate markets. The condition for arbitrage is that the profit is "risk-free." Such profits tend to be very temporary in nature because in efficient markets those opportunities get quickly arbitraged away. There are many examples of arbitrage. A stock trading on one exchange with its price of out of sync to its corresponding futures contract on another exchange, an arbitrageur would sell short the expensive security (futures contract) and buy the stock. The profit is the difference between stock price and the futures price. For that profit to not exist (no arbitrage) there are three conditions that should be met:

1. The security has to trade at the same price on all markets.
2. Two securities that have identical features such as cash flow, dividend or coupon/maturity, have to trade at the same price.
3. A futures contract price is equal to the cash security price discounted by the risk free rate. In other words, the forward price of a stock is the same as the futures price of that stock.

In bond switching, there is often a case of arbitrage. Specifically, in government bonds where two securities close in maturity and coupon could trade at a different price. This is also known as relative-value arbitrage. This form of arbitrage relies on a strong correlation between two related or unrelated securities. It is primarily used during sideways markets as a way to make profit of tiny price differentials. In stocks, correlation is more important than in bonds. Highly correlated stock prices based on history may present more perfect pairs than in bonds. That is because bonds have maturity and duration differences. A correlation between bonds is often associated with credit risk. When a correlation turns negative, that may imply a bond from a certain issuer has a higher risk of a credit downgrade or an increased level of default risk. The fine line is liquidity. Arbitrage success relies greatly on minimizing transaction costs, speed of execution, and access to liquidity. An arbitrage may on paper look attractive, but in reality can be deceiving if liquidity is poor and ability to execute is diminished. An arbitrage is to find pairs of stocks that correlate positively, but where bonds may correlate negatively. The bonds are at the upper end of the "capital structure." That means they are senior to equity, which is at the lower end of the capital structure. There is an arbitrage when the stock versus bond correlation deviates.

For example, if JP Morgan and Bank of America stock have a positive correlation of 0.9, a stock investor could arbitrage the price difference if there is a divergence from where historically both stocks have traded relative to one another. A bond investor would arbitrage the yield spread or option-adjusted spread differential because of minor coupon and maturity. When approached from a cross-over point of view, the arbitrage becomes a function of correlation difference between stocks and bonds. When that correlation difference has deviated from history, there is an opportunity to switch from stocks to bonds. This would also be the case because a negative correlation in bonds implies a change in risk perception that may not necessarily be implied by the stock correlation. In the example of JP Morgan (JPM) and Bank of America (BofA), the JPM stock price correlation using weekly data was 0.85 versus BofA. The JPM bond correlation was 0.1 to BofA bonds. That may suggest that, because JPM and BofA are fairly similar in activity and scope, JPM bonds could be relatively attractive to BofA bonds, while the stocks may say the opposite. The "arbitrage" would be to sell JPM stock versus BofA and buy JPM bonds versus BofA. The gain or loss would be expressed by the difference in prices where the investor has a price convergence target. A different way of looking at this trade is to assess the valuation of the capital structure. If an investor sells JPM stock for BofA and does the opposite with bonds, then what an investor really is arbitraging is the dividend and coupon differences. That is a more fundamental arbitrage by judging the components of the capital structure being under- or overvalued based on the expectation of coupon and dividend payments.

3
Equity Strategy for the Bond Investor

In the analysis of stocks, traditional multiples like enterprise to earnings before interest and taxes (EV/EBITDA), PE, PB, and price to sales (P/S) on an absolute basis and a relative basis play a pivotal role. An equity relative value analysis compares stocks that trade at a deep discount to book value or, for example, at a high premium to earnings. Moreover, a convincing signal, whether a stock is a buy or a sell, is when the stock trades at discount or premium in many of the mentioned financial ratios. Before such a relative value analysis can be done, the investor has to do bottom-up research. A stock investor should first look at forward earnings to test sensitivities based on the operating and financial leverage in order to identify the risk and reward. This is one of the most important concepts for valuation—to have confidence in one or more scenarios within a range of reasonable multiples. It is, however, impossible to look at the multiple on forward earnings without understanding the assumptions of those earnings estimations. To get the assumptions right is an important part of the valuation process. For more cyclical businesses, it can make sense to normalize the earnings over a longer term. A more accurate measure would be to estimate at what point of the cycle the business is operating. An early-cycle business might not get the benefits of multiple expansions relative to the market's PE expansion. Industry dynamics that could translate to companies' future plans and longer-term earnings power can be discounted back. Combined, they determine the sum of fair value today. The discounted cash flow model is often used in these instances as a sanity check on assumptions such as long-term margins, sales, and expected embedded interest rates.

The most important tool for valuation in the short term (three to six months) is trying to understand the earnings model and where current EPS/revenue estimates or other key value driving estimates are for a particular company or stock. A sufficient effort in research and modeling is required to come up with a variant view to the consensus research. The research output is likely to drive the stock in a much more consistent and attributable fashion because earnings expectations in and of themselves are used in consensus models for valuation. The revisions of higher or lower value will ultimately drive the stock with a greater probability than compared to any other part of the process of stock valuation. In other words, analysts can have a view of which valuation metric is right or wrong, and whether it is a high or low PE ratio. When there is no strong market expectation for these valuation metrics, company earnings estimates that are widely followed are a very clear benchmark for determining intrinsic value. In theory, a stock's intrinsic value is an estimate of what the stock is really worth as opposed to the value traded in the market. If the intrinsic value is more than the current share price, the stock is worth more, and that would support a buy recommendation.

Intrinsic value is determined by a company's sum of its discounted cash flows. The sum of cash flows measures what a company is worth in terms of its future profits. These future profits must be discounted to account for the time value of money. The time value of money is the force by which the one dollar received in one year's time is worth less than a dollar earned today. The case for intrinsic value to equal a company's future profits is directly related to the value proposition of the business to the stakeholders. A business represents profits, which is generally measured by the difference between revenues and costs. The profit generated by a business is the basis of intrinsic value of a company. Table 3.1 shows a simplistic version of the intrinsic value of a hypothetical company. Finance textbooks often use such examples, but in reality stocks are not traded based on these models. Intrinsic valuation is an estimate of fair value under a set of assumptions. Those assumptions may help shape the view on the level of a stock price.

The model in Table 3.1 uses a prior-year cash flow. This the total profits that the shareholders could take from the

Table 3.1   Intrinsic value model

	Year 1	Year 2	Year 3	Year 4	Year 5
Prior year cash flow	$ 100.00	$ 115.00	$ 132.00	$ 152.00	$ 175.00
Growth Rate	15%	15%	15%	15%	15%
Cash Flow	$ 115.00	$ 132.25	$ 151.80	$ 174.80	$ 201.25
Discount factor	0.93	0.86	0.79	0.74	0.68
Discount value per year	$ 106.00	$ 113.00	$ 121.00	$ 129.00	$ 137.00
Total sum of cash flows					606
Residual value					
Cash flow in five years	201				
Growth rate	5%				
Cash flow in six years	$ 211.20				
Capitalization rate	3%				
Value at year 5	7039				
Discount rate at year 5	0.68				
PV of residual	$ 4,791.00				
Intrinsic value of company	$ 5,397.00				

Source: Author, hypothetical example.

company in the previous year. The assumed growth rate is the rate at which the owner's earnings are expected to grow for the next five years. The cash flow is the amount that shareholders would get if all the company's profits were distributed to them. By discounting the cash flow with a discount rate, the computed number brings the future cash flows back to the starting year. That is the year in which the discounted future cash flow determines the company's present value (PV). The capitalization rate is the discount rate (the denominator). The discount rate can be derived from financing rates obtained in the marketplace. Table 3.1 shows what the company is theoretically worth and what the fair value of the stock should be.

In markets, stocks are not treated as discounted cash flows but rather as trading opportunities. In the "greater fool theory," the distinction between profit and present vale plays an important role. Since the profit on a trade is not determined by a company's value, it is about speculating whether a person can sell the (overvalued) stock to another investor (the fool). However, a trader would say that investors who rely solely on fundamentals, would ignore important trends in the market. There is always a greater fool who buys a stock for its fundamental or intrinsic value. There is a case for managers to abide by intrinsic valuation because there are several variants.

An intrinsic valuation model based on a single-stage earnings discount model could value the S&P 500 Index based on consensus EPS estimates. Another method is to use the dividend discount model (DDM) or a discounted cash flow (DCF) model with the direct input of EPS. In a dividend growth or free cash flow discount model, future cash flows can be discounted directly. However, earnings growth cannot be discounted directly because earnings growth fails to account for what portion of prior period earnings were retained. Thus, an EPS discount model must separate EPS growth into two parts: 1) growth from reinvestment at returns equal to the cost of equity and 2) growth from returns in excess of the cost of equity or economic profit growth. An EPS discount model calculates intrinsic value by taking the present value of growth in economic profits (not ordinary profits) and adds this to the capitalized value of current normalized EPS. Once economic profit growth stops, equity value is simply EPS capitalized at the real cost of equity. This is because EPS growth only adds to steady-state value when EPS growth is greater than the retention ratio times the real cost of equity. To calculate the fair value of the PE multiple on a normalized EPS, one takes the reciprocal of a long-term stock return adjusted for inflation. If the sum of the long-term EPS growth rate and dividend yield is equal to the real cost of equity, then a company operates in a "steady state.". The steady state is the "ideal world" where the market value of the stock trades close to intrinsic value.

In a steady state context, to determine how much a business is worth, three questions must be answered: 1) What are the normalized and accounting quality adjusted earnings? 2) What is a fair rate at which to capitalize such normalized earnings? and 3) Can the business replicate itself and increase its economic profits? Stock analysts often look at the normalized EPS for short-term stock performance. In reality investors should look at the actual EPS through the full business cycle to judge long-term stock performance. The most widely used metric for stock valuation is the PE ratio. The PE ratio is driven by normalized EPS and intrinsic value, and any uncertainty by analysts' estimates surrounding these numbers. To avoid that noise creeping into investors' judgment, valuing normalized EPS and economic profits requires a cost-of-equity and cost-of-debt estimate.

The cost of equity is the long-term "risk-free" interest rate plus an equity risk premium. The cost of debt is the weighted average interest rate at which corporate debt can be issued. Together they form the weighted average cost of capital (WACC), a yardstick for any stock analyst to determine whether a company generates enough free cash flow in excess of the weighted average cost of capital or whether it destroys its profit capacity. The WACC can be a useful measure to estimate in real time the relative valuation of the debt and equity portion of a company's market value. When modeling intrinsic value, there can also a WACC implied. The difference between the actual WACC and the WACC implied from intrinsic value provides a measure of "fair value" of the capital structure in its entirety. Breaking down the intrinsic model as a broad measure for the "fair value" of a stock, lists a number of items a stock picker should look at when analyzing the shares of a particular company:

- Share price should be no more than two-thirds of its intrinsic value.
- Companies should have PE ratios at the lowest 10 percent of all equity securities in their peer group.
- Stock price should be no more than tangible book value.
- Debt-to-equity ratio is preferably below 100.
- Current assets should be two times current liabilities.
- Dividend yield should be at least two-thirds of the long-term government bond yield.
- Earnings growth should be at least 7 percent per annum compounded over the last ten years (Ibbotson research).

The same list could be created for a company's debt based off the intrinsic model. The corporate bonds outstanding should not represent more than 50 percent of the market capitalization of the company. Corporate debt maturities should be well spread out in time. If a company has a too botched "maturity wall" of debt coming due in one to three years time, there is high roll-over risk. A company that has sufficient access to capital markets to get competitive funding for ten years is a healthy sign. An appropriate use of leverage through debt issuance that has an average maturity of ten to twenty years will benefit the stability of earnings and thereby create long-run value for the stock holder.

Growth and Value

The list above is not a precise framework for stock valuation. Value investors seek stocks with normalized earnings greater than market expectations. Growth investors seek stocks with economic profit growth. The first question a growth investor should ask is whether the company, based on annual revenue, has been growing in the past. Below in Table 3.2 are rough guidelines for the rate of EPS growth an investor should look for in companies of differing sizes, which would indicate their growth investing potential.

For example, an established large cap company will not be able to grow as quickly as a younger small-cap tech company. Also, when evaluating analyst consensus estimates,

Table 3.2 Approximate growth rates for companies

Company market cap	Minimum historical growth rate
More than 4 billion	5%–8%
Between 400MM and 4bn	7%–11%
Less than 400MM	12%–20%

Source: S&P, Ibbotson, Investopedia. A second criterion for stock selection is a projected five-year growth rate of at least 10%–12%, although 15% or more is ideal. These projections are made by analysts, the company, or other credible sources. The big problem with forward estimates is that they are estimates. When a growth investor sees an ideal growth projection, he or she, before trusting this projection, must evaluate its credibility. This requires knowledge of the typical growth rates for different sizes of companies.

an investor should learn about the company's industry, specifically, what its prospects are and what stage of growth it is at. A third guideline is pretax profit margins. There are many examples of companies with high growth in sales but moderate growth in earnings. High annual revenue growth is good, but if EPS has not increased proportionately, it is likely due to a decrease in profit margin. By comparing a company's present profit margins to its past margins and its competition's profit margins, a growth investor is able to gauge fairly accurately whether or not management is controlling costs and revenues and maintaining margins. A good rule of thumb is that if company exceeds its previous five-year average of pretax profit margins as well as those of its industry, the company may be a good growth candidate. Efficiency can be quantified by using ROE. Efficient use of assets should be reflected in a stable or increasing ROE. The analysis of this metric should be relative: a company's present ROE is best compared to the five-year average ROE of the company and the industry. If a stock cannot realistically double in five years, it is probably not a growth stock. So the rate growth investors are seeking is high—perhaps 15 percent per annum—which yields in a potential doubling in price in five years.

Capital Structure

A company's capital structure—essentially, its blend of equity and debt financing—is a significant factor in determining the value of a business. The relative levels of equity and debt affect risk and cash flow and, therefore, the amount an investor would be willing to pay for the company's shares. A question that often arises is whether the valuator should use the company's actual capital structure or its anticipated future capital structure. A valuator might also use a prospective buyer's capital structure or the company's optimal capital structure. Determining which method is best depends on several factors, including the type of stakeholder's interest being valued and the valuation's purpose itself. Capital structure matters because it influences the cost of capital. Generally, when valuators use income-based valuation methods—such as discounted cash flow—they convert projected cash flows or other economic benefits to present value by applying a present value discount rate. That discount rate, which generally reflects the return that a hypothetical investor would require, is derived from the cost of capital, which is commonly based on the weighted average cost of capital (WACC). WACC is a company's average cost of equity and debt, weighted according to the relative proportion of each in the company's capital structure.

Many business owners strive to be debt free, but a reasonable amount of debt can provide some financial benefits. Debt is often cheaper than equity, and interest payments are tax deductible. So, as the level of debt increases, returns to equity owners also increase—enhancing the company's value. If risk were not a factor, then the more debt a business had, the greater its value would be. But at a certain level of debt, the risks associated with higher leverage begin to outweigh the financial advantages. When debt reaches this point, investors may demand higher returns as compensation for taking on greater risk, which has a negative impact on business value. Therefore, the optimal capital structure comprises a sufficient level of debt to maximize investor returns without incurring excessive risk. Identifying the optimal structure is a combination of art and science. Valuators may therefore:

1. Use industry averages,
2. Examine capital structures of guideline companies,

3. Refer to financial institutions' debt-to-equity lending criteria,

4. Apply financial models to estimate a subject company's optimal structure.

Whichever method is used, valuators exercise professional judgment to arrive at a capital structure that makes sense for the subject company, with a level of debt that the company's cash flow can support. If the interest being valued is a controlling interest, it is often appropriate to use the company's optimal capital structure. A controlling owner generally has the ability to change the company's capital structure and gravitates toward a structure that will yield the most profitable results. If the interest being valued is a minority or noncontrolling interest, however, it is customary to use the company's actual capital structure, because the interest owner lacks that ability.

To estimate fair market value, analysts use a company's actual or optimal capital structure. A company's capital structure fluctuates over time as the value of its equity securities changes and the company pays down debt. It may be appropriate to use management's target capital structure if the actual structure deviated off course or if management plans to alter the company's capital structure. A changing mix of debt and equity can have a big impact on a value estimate of the optimal capital structure.

There are several methods to determine the "optimal" capital structure of a particular company. By researching statistics from sources such as Ibbotson, rating agencies like Standard & Poor's, or investment bank research, the operational assumption is companies in related industries are at an optimal capital structure. The industry statistics on the cost of capital may provide the comfort of a benchmark, but it would be too easy to assume these are applicable to the specific company in question. There is also an issue concerning what time horizon the cost of capital statistics have been computed that may conflict with the time horizon of the valuation of a company. There are therefore different ways to estimate the optimal capital structure.

An investor can analyze the average or median capital structure of companies operating in the same sector. The similarity in operational activity, companies in the same sector can provide a guideline. The caveat is that market price fluctuations and random issuance of debt, may cause a deviation between the median and target capital structure. In a larger set of guideline companies, the median capital structure can become a more solid average, and better reflects the optimal capital structure. Another drawback of the optimal capital structure is companies that operate near optimal, may be incentivized to issue more corporate debt. That could increase the risk of the capital structure overall, and so an appropriate risk premium is added to the rate of return on debt and equity, to compensate the stakeholders for the additional risk. When incorporating risk premium, the more complex version of the optimal capital structure is one that has a "cost of capital curve." This curve is not the same as the yield curve, but rather the cost of capital curve illustrates a company's weighted average cost of capital by simulating different combinations of debt and equity funding. In his book, *The Dark Side of Valuation*, Aswath Damodaran of New York University's Stern School of Business discusses the capital cost curve in more detail.

The cost of capital has two components, namely debt and equity. The cost of debt is mainly determined by market interest rates, default probabilities and tax deductibility. The cost of debt is less straightforward than what is commonly assumed. The debt service ratio is a relevant measure to assess a company's appropriate level of debt relative to its free cash flow and credit rating. Based on the debt service coverage, a synthetic rating can be determined in order to apply an average default spread for each part of debt of the capital structure. The default spread can be derived from market-observed spreads, since the (synthetic) ratings are generally applied to large publicly traded companies. The cost of equity can also be implied from the capital cost curve. The cost of equity is generally driven by the company's stock beta and debt-to-equity ratio. When applied to the capital asset pricing model (CAPM), the levered beta are used to estimate the cost of equity at different levels of debt. Once the simulation of the capital structure is completed, the WACC for each debt level is calculated. The optimal capital structure would be the structure in which the WACC is the lowest. A more consistently lower WACC would keep the value of the firm at higher levels when the expected cash flows are discounted at the lower WACC.

Putting Theory into Practice

The relative value between stocks and bonds can be approached by two sets of models. The capital structure model is based on the original ideas of Modigliani and Miller. Their groundbreaking work was published in 1963 in *the American Economic Review* under the title "Corporate income taxes and the cost of capital: a correction." The other model is to assess the value of convertible bonds and convertible capital notes. The analysis in the following sections focuses on valuing the lower end of the capital structure, the part where debt and equity are closely related. In general, there is a relationship between equity value and corporate debt value. An approach to show that is the case, is to regress the S&P 500 Index and the Investment Grade CDX Index (IG CDX series). Figure 3.1 show how there is a decent relationship between the S&P and CDX. When the S&P 500 declines in value, the IG CDX widens in risk premium and vice versa. The inverse relationship says that the value of debt and equity in the capital structure can be close in times of financial stress. When default expectations rise, a company's capital structure "flattens." That means its senior unsecured debt is priced like equity. At other times when equity prices rise, senior debt can trade at a very tight risk premiums. That is caused by very low default probability as well as the ample access to capital markets. Figure 3.1 shows that the capital structure of an index exhibits a correlation between the cost of debt and the cost of equity. This analysis can be taken to the company level.

A comparison of capital structures like, for example, IBM and Apple, can show why there can be significant differences in risk premiums of debt and equity between companies, as well as valuation because of different levels of

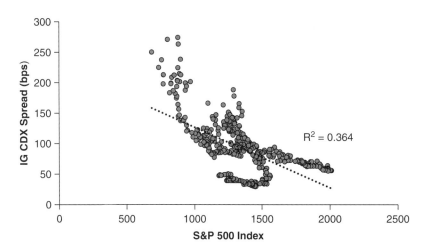

Figure 3.1 IG CDX an S&P 500 Index.
Source: Yahoo Finance, FRB, weekly data, 2003–2014.

debt. Each company is valued based upon the expectation of future profits, the amount of debt financing that is used and an assessment of the overall macroeconomic environment. The capital structure model is a calculation that addresses those three elements. Tables 3.3 through 3.6 show the cases of IBM versus Apple. A conclusion from the model output for both companies is that Apple stock price would have been 6 percent higher than the market price (at the time of writing in 2014) if the company had a higher debt-to-capital ratio and a lower WACC. For IBM, the stock price was undervalued relative to the optimal capital structure because it had a too high debt-to-capital ratio. In real time, the capital structure of Apple and IBM may be trading closer because markets assign equal default probabilities to the companies because of each strength of their balance sheets. To determine whether that is the case, a more practical application of the capital structure model is needed.

The capital structure model by New York University Stern School of Business is such a practical version for addressing the issues of the "optimal" capital structure. Tables 3.3 through 3.6 show how, with inputs from financial statements, the optimal capital structure can be practically estimated. The important question is how the optimal capital

Table 3.3 IBM capital structure

	IBM Current	IBM Optimal
Debt to Capital	0.13	0.1
Cost of capital	7.42%	7.34%
Enterprise value	$ 199,208.80	$ 201,925.47
Value per share	182.05	184.77

*Value as of September 2014.

structure has been determined, and which component (debt or equity) is under- or overvalued (or appropriately valued). The analysis from Table 3.3 indicates the equity component of IBM is somewhat "undervalued" relative to the optimal capital structure. By adjusting the WACC and the debt-to-capital/debt-to-equity ratio, the "fair value" of the debt can be derived. A capital structure model allows the investor to compare the current equity and debt valuation to what the model says is "optimal." Of course, what is optimal may seem like theory. In reality, markets do price in options and credit default swaps what the intrinsic value (optimal value) is versus the current value. The inputs in Table 3.4 calculate what the value of the company's shares are based on the overall cost of capital.

Table 3.4 IBM input

IBM Capital structure model	Inputs
EBITDA	$ 6,081
Depreciation & Amortization	$ 3,327
Capital Spending	$ 3,806
Interest debt expense	29
Marginal Tax Rate	15.5%
Bond Rating	A1/A+
Pretax cost of debt	3.63%
Number of shares outstanding (min)	997
Market price/share	$ 182.05
IBM beta	0.9
Book value of debt	$ 30,120.00
Assumed "risk-free" rate	2%
CAPM risk premium	6%
Country default probability	0.30%

Source: Ashwath Damodaran, New York University Stern School of Business. Numbers as reported by GAAP FY 2013. Model found at http://pages.stern.nyu.edu/~adamodar/ under optimal capital structure.

For IBM, the term structure of its debt—the average maturities of its issued bonds—is up to 30 years. IBM's CDS curve has maturities out to ten years. With its average debt maturity at six years, there is a point at which the value of IBM's bonds and its stock cross over. The capital structure of IBM shows the idea. The difference between the current and the optimal capital structure is shown in Table 3.3. In the table, the capital structure difference can be seen from the difference between the enterprise values as well as the weighted average costs of capital. For IBM, the difference in WACC under the current and optimal structure is eight basis points (namely, 7.42 percent to 7.34 percent). By multiplying the eight basis points times the average maturity of the debt (six years), the premium in unit of risk for the optimal capital structure is worth 48 basis points (or 0.48 percent). The value of IBM's five-year CDS was around 42 basis points at the time of writing (fall 2014). The CDS premium being lower than the optimal structure premium may suggest IBM's debt was trading at a slightly too tight risk premium. Another way of looking at this analysis is to multiply the eight basis points by the average duration of IBM's corporate bonds, which was about 5.7 years of duration. In price percentage points, this is about 4.5 percent "overvaluation" (5.7 years * 8 basis points) of IBM's debt. What Table 3.3 shows, in contrast, is that IBM's stock was about 1.5 percent (182.05 vs. 184.77 optimal) "undervalued." The analysis of the capital structure shows that, by valuing both debt and equity at the optimal level, the fair valuation of debt and equity in the current capital structure can be determined.

When analyzing Apple stock, it appears from Table 3.5 on page 111 that it is a different story. By early 2015, Apple stock was trading at around $118/share. In February 2015,

Table 3.5 Apple capital structure

	Current	Optimal
Debt to Capital	4%	35%
Cost of capital	6%	7%
Enterprise value (mlns)	$ 731,452.78	$ 659,443.09
Value per share	$ 118.00	$ 101.90

Value as of February 2015.

Apple issued a new series of notes with maturities from 5 years to 30 years. The average yield on the bonds was around 1.5 percent to 3.5 percent across the different maturities. As a result, Apple's cost of capital was very much lower (6 percent) than what the optimal model may suggest. More importantly, Apple was not using leverage more efficiently. Rather, the company was sitting on a large cash balance (reportedly $160 billion) that was used to buy back its shares to return the cash to the shareholders by a higher stock price. The capital structure looks to be imbalanced, with the stock "overvalued" relative to Apple bonds. The capital structure output provides a conclusion what should is "optimal" in a perfect world. In practice, it would be quite unlikely that we would see a sharp fall in Apple stock price without other factors like profitability and earnings playing an important role.

The examples of IBM and Apple show how a model can provide a careful estimate of the relative valuation of stocks and bonds within a company's market capitalization. Critical are the assumptions of the capital structure model. When a company has sufficient cash, it can use leverage by issuing debt, which can optimize the capital structure. The model should be seen as one of the checks in an investor's assessment of the equity and debt risk of a particular company.

Table 3.6 Apple Inputs

Apple Capital structure model	Inputs (in mlns)
EBITDA	$ 55,757
Depreciation & Amortization	$ 5,800
Capital Spending	$ 7,700
Interest debt expense	$ 20.00
Marginal Tax Rate (%)	26.0%
Bond Rating	A2/A
Pretax cost of debt	2.50%
Number of shares oustanding	5987
Market price/share	$ 97.20
Apple beta to S&P	0.83
Book value of debt	$ 31,040.00
Assumed "risk-free" rate	2%
CAPM risk premium	7%
Country default probability	0.30%

Source: Ashwath Damodaran, New York University Stern School of Business. Numbers as reported by GAAP FY 2013/Bloomberg data. Model found at http://pages.stern.nyu.edu/~adamodar/ under optimal capital structure.

The Magic of Alibaba

Another example of the capital structure analysis is Alibaba. The Alibaba Group is the largest e-commerce platform in the world, as measured by gross merchandise volume (GMV), which was 253 billion USD in 2013. This is 1.2 times larger than Amazon, 2.3 times larger than eBay, and 11 times larger than JD.com. Its Tmall (business-to-consumer) and Taobao (consumer-to-consumer) platforms had a combined 80 percent market share in China's e-commerce sector in 2013. Based in the most populated country in the world—China—Alibaba has immense scale, including 1 billion in product and services listing, 8.5 million annual active sellers, and 307 million annual active buyers. During its largest promotional event on Singles

Day (November 11) 2014, a record $9.3 billion of GMV was settled through Alipay. This is Alibaba's escrow payment system, similar to the IPO, in which the stock was launched at 68 dollars/share and soared to 93 dollars/share. In November 2014 the company came to market with an 8 billion-dollar corporate bond issue. The corporate bond issue was part of the financing of the IPO. Table 3.7 shows what the new corporate bond issue looked like.

In terms of credit fundamentals, Alibaba's agency model is one in which it only provides the platform, with no inventory risk. Most of its revenue comes from performance-based marketing services and display advertisement. Margins are high, with its large-scale and asset-lite nature—operating margin was 42 percent for Alibaba compared to 18 percent for eBay, 27 percent for Google, and an operating loss for Amazon. Alibaba generates significant free cash flow given the agency model. Alibaba is not exposed to any sourcing or inventory risks, and is in partnership with 14 logistics companies for its logistics network. The Company has a net

Table 3.7 Comparison valuation of Alibaba's corporate bonds

Tranche	3yr Fixed/FRN	5yr Fixed/FRN	7yr Fixed
Expected Size	ca. US$1.5bn	ca. US$2.5bn	ca. US$1bn
Initial Price Talk	T3+ 80bps	T5 + 110bps	T7+ 135bps
Expected Pricing Level	T3 + 67.5bps	T5 + 95bps	T7 + 120bps
LOAS	46bps	80bps	111bps
YTM	1.64%	2.68%	3.25%
Spread Duration	2.96yr	4.73yr	6.28yr
China CDS	41/44	83/85	110/118
Orderbooks	3yr Fix: $4bn	5yr Fix: $7bn	7yr Fix: $7.25bn
	3yr FRN: $1.3bn	5yr FRN: $1.5bn	

Source: SEC.
The 3yr and 5yr **FRN were priced at the Libor-equivalent levels of their respective fixed tranches.

cash position of 9.7 billion dollars post its IPO, a pro forma total leverage of 1.71 times, and net leverage of 2.03 times. The Company is committed to keeping its net cash position and is observant of a net leverage ratio of 1.5 times, which is appropriate for its A+ rating. Against the projection of free cash flow expansion and net debt to EBITDA remaining negative in 2017, the newly issued corporate bonds had attractive value versus Alibaba's stock.

Crossover investing would compare the value of the new issued bonds to comparable issuers. In Table 3.8, the Alibaba bonds are compared to other issuers. At first glance, the Alibaba issue is "cheaper" on an OAS spread basis versus issuers like Cisco (CSCO), which has a similar rating. The Alibaba securities have longer duration and are therefore at a higher yield and wider OAS spread. How about Alibaba's bond valuation versus the stock valuation? The capital structure model would say that because of Alibaba's low leverage and surge in stock price, the Alibaba bonds would have some value. That should also be a function of Alibaba's low cost of capital.

A different comparison than the capital structure model is to look at Alibaba's earnings yield implied by the stock versus the yield on Alibaba's bonds. Table 3.9 on page 115 shows

Table 3.8 Alibaba bond comparison

Bond	Rating	Yield (%)	OAS spread (bps)	Spread duration (yr)
Alibaba 5yr	A1/A+/A+	2.58%	80	4.73
Cisco 5yr	A1/AA–/NR	2.03%	45	4.14
eBay 5yr	A2/A/A–	2.25%	55	4.46
GLW 5yr	A3/A–/A–	2.27%	66	4.2
Bidu 5yr	A3/NR/A	2.78%	113	4.31

Source: SEC, FRB.

Table 3.9 Earnings yield versus bond yield

	Alibaba	
	Current	**Hist Avg**
NTM P/E	40.6x	36.9x
Earnings Yield	2.46%	2.71%
Alibaba New 5y	2.68%	2.68%

Source: SEC.

that comparison. The 20 basis points difference between the earnings yield and the bond yield says that the risk premium for Alibaba's stock was very low. The yield on five-year US Treasury bond were at around 1.65 percent at the time of issuance of Alibaba's corporate bonds. Alibaba's equity risk premium was worth about 80 basis points, or 0.8 percent. This is calculated by taking the difference between Alibaba's stock earnings yield minus the yield on five year Treasury bond. The equity risk premium for Alibaba was low compared to the S&P 500 Index equity risk premium that was around 4 percent (when using the S&P 500 earnings yield minus the Treasury yield). This risk premium comparison also suggested that Alibaba bonds had value relative to Alibaba's stock around the time of the IPO. In general, a basic comparison like the one in Table 3.9 can be done for any stock to identify value relative to debt.

Convertible Bonds

A convertible bond is a security that the investor can convert into common stock by way of a conversion ratio. A convertible bond is probably the best example of the cross-over strategy. It is a hybrid security that has both bond and stock features, and therefore trades with higher volatility than a bond. The reason for volatility is the conversion option, which is why the convertible bond has a lower coupon than regular bonds. The unique feature is the upside with limited downside. An investor in a convertible bond has the opportunity to convert into shares should the stock rise or continue to collect the regular coupon payments and principle return at maturity. Specialized strategies such as merger or convertible arbitrage directly relate to the conversion option that is a combination of a long position in the convertible bond with a short position in the underlying stock. Convertible bond models are quite complex. There are several assumptions that go along with valuing a convertible bond. There are basic models available online where the conversion option value can be computed. The value of conversion is what makes convertible bonds unique to other bonds. In the following subsections, there are two examples discussed—Twitter and Dynegy. In each case there is convertible bond valuation put into practice.

The case of Twitter

When Twitter (TWTR) became IPO, the company took its global online platform for public self-expression to a new level. As of the three months ended on June 30, 2014, Twitter had 271 million monthly active users, spanning nearly every country. The most-followed Twitter users are Katy Perry and Justin Bieber, with the president of the United States coming in a distant third. In the summer of 2014, TWTR came to market with a 1.3 billion-dollar convertible debt deal. The deal consisted out of two tranches: a five-year and seven-year maturity, plus a "green shoe" (15%) in case of more investor demand (a green shoe is an option to issue more bonds). The proceeds would be used for general corporate purposes. At the time, the price talk for each $650 million tranche was 0.25 percent yield for the five-year and 1.00 percent for the seven-year bond. The

Table 3.10   Twitter convertible bond valuation

5-year bond			7-year bond		
Volatility (%)	Model OAS	OAS	Volatility (%)	Model OAS	OAS
30	69	57	30	69	57
35	158	141	35	158	141
40	252	235	40	252	235
45	349	310	45	349	310

Source: Yahoo Finance, SEC. Modeled spread is calculated by inputting the different spreads as strikes in Table 3.10 under the different volatility assumptions.

bonds were modeled on a theoretical sum-of-parts valuation (capital structure model, as discussed earlier) and using assumptions for longer-dated equity implied volatility (see associated Table 3.10). At a closing price for the stock of $52.91 in the fall of 2014, the conversion price would have been $78.04. Notwithstanding the (theoretical) "cheapness" described above, at best, the convertible bond was at fair value in 2014, given the company's elevated valuation metrics—like an EV/EBIDTA of 31.3x and a price/sales ratio of 9.7x. While the company may have been in the early stages of monetizing its platform, the uncertainty surrounding how much revenue the company could extract from its user base remained significant.

The Case of Dynegy

Dynegy (DYN) is an independent utility that acquired Duke Energy's PJM merchant fleet for $2.8 billion. This was 6.7x estimated 2015 EBITDA. The acquisition of Energy Capital Partner's PJM (Mid-Atlantic) and New England merchant fleet was worth about $3.45 billion and 6.2x estimated 2015 EBITDA. The transaction was expected to close by the end of 1Q15. Dynegy's pro forma gross leverage increased from 4.6x (as of 2Q 2014) to 5.3x (estimated for 2015). The higher leverage and increased debt-to-enterprise value were more than offset by the benefit of increased scale and diversity. Also, Dynegy generated a greater percentage of cash flow from capacity payments (25% of 2015 gross margin versus 11% for Dynegy standalone). As a result, the volatility of the business was meaningfully reduced. Dynegy's "legacy coal" (as opposed to the new clean coal technologies) was scheduled to retire in June 2017, and comprised approximately 6 percent of the pro forma energy generation capacity. To fund the takeover of PJM, three senior debt tranches were issued for a total of $5 billion. The balance of $1.1 billion was funded by DYN equity and convertible bond offerings.

To facilitate the acquisition, a $5.3 billion Dynegy Bridge loan was issued. This was a key financing commitment for Dynegy's acquisition of two power plant portfolios. The bridge loan was expected to be taken out within a month through new bond issuance. As part of the transaction Dynegy raised $1 billion–$1.5 billion of equity and issued new convertible bonds to replace the bridge loan. In terms of specifics regarding the convertible bonds, Dynegy provided the following details to investors:

1. All-in cap rate for seven-year noncallable after three years security of 8 percent. This set the "strike" for the convertible option at 534 basis points OAS. Part of the deal was the "strike" steps up to 592 basis points OAS by February 2015. When compared to existing Dynegy 2023 maturity bonds, those were trading at an OAS of 362 basis points at the time.
2. The bridge loan was likely to expire within one month for a commitment fee of 75 basis points. The assumed implied volatility was 116 percent.

The valuation of this convertible deal at different levels of the OAS spread and volatility produces a conversion value. Because Dynegy's offering came during a time in October of 2014 when market volatility suddenly rose sharply, the conversion value ranged from $1.76 to as high as $36. That, compared to Dynegy's stock price in October of 2014 at around the $28–$32 range, indicated the convertible bond deal had some value. The convertible bond market is a good indication of how markets are pricing the capital structure of a Dynegy.

In the fall of 2014, Dynegy issued ten-year bonds at a 7.5 percent yield for $1.25 billion of notes in total at a coupon of 7.625 percent. The biggest portion of Dynegy's offering was $2.1 billion of five-year notes that yielded 6.75 percent. The company also offered $1.75 billion of 7.375 percent, eight-year securities. The bond proceeds were also part of the financing for the $6.25 billion acquisition of coal and gas-fired generation assets from Duke Energy. Possibly because of the convertible option, the coupons of the new issue Dynegy bonds were 1.5 percent higher than the outstanding Dynegy bonds. The convertible bond deal range valuation indicated that the actual bonds were relatively undervalued to Dynegy's stock. This is specifically the case when volatility experiences a sharp rise. In general, when equity volatility goes up, convertible bonds can see a decline in market value.

In terms of general investment opportunities in convertible bonds, there are several funds available. One of the more popular ones is the SPDR ® Barclays Convertible Securities ETF. This ETF is benchmarked off the Barclays US Convertible Bond Index, which is designed to represent the market of US convertible securities, such as convertible bonds. The ETF tends to closely track the S&P 500 Index albeit with some lag on a total return basis, shown by Figure 3.2 on page 120.

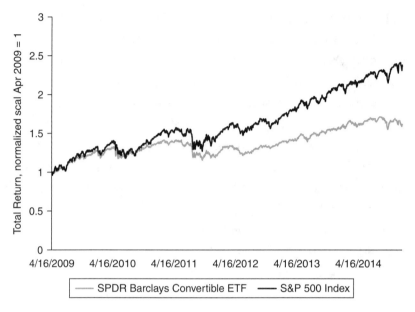

Figure 3.2 S&P 500 vs. SPDR Convertible Bond ETF Total Return is after fees.
Source: FRB, March 2009–December 2014.

The convertible bond market is small, with just $450 billion total outstanding, and is not always accessible to the general public. It is market in which an investor, by using a volatility assumption of a broader index like S&P 500 or the Volatility Index on the Chicago Board of Trade, can calculate the cross-over value between stocks and bonds. The convertibility factor became an important feature for bank debt in the wake of recapitalization after the financial crisis. "CoCos" are the new innovation of crossover between stocks and bonds. In the sections that follow, each of the fixed income sectors that have much in common with equity will be discussed.

Equity-Like Debt: Contingent Convertible Capital Instruments ("CoCos") and Subordinated Debt

In the capital structure of a company, subordinated debt is junior to senior creditors. In case of a bankruptcy or liquidation, subordinated debt gets wiped out along with the equity holders. The status of subordinated debt is therefore called "junior debt." The reason why debt is referred to as "subordinate" is because the debt holders have subordinated claims on a company relative to the senior debt holders, the liquidator, and government tax agencies. That means subordinated debt holders will only be paid after all senior debt holders have been paid. A liquidation or bankruptcy entails likely haircuts on principal of the debt outstanding, in general, after all senior holders are paid, the subordinated bond holders get back very little. Investing in subordinated debt is risky and has equity characteristics in terms of price volatility and voting rights. Subordinated debt has a low rating and is traded at higher yield than investment-grade debt. Subordinated bonds can be issued alongside a public initial offer of a stock. A trade-off to subordinated debt is a direct equity capital injection, but sub debt can also be used as part of the capital injection. This form of debt injection happens in the financial sector. Banks in particular are frequent issuers of subordinated debt whereby that part of the capital structure is risk sensitive because of the junior status to other debt holders. The purpose of sub debt can be because of "market discipline" reasons, enticed by bank regulators to disincentive moral hazard. An investment portfolio strategy focused on subordinated bonds might be used as a substitute for a bank stock portfolio. The reason is that capital securities have historically provided better risk-adjusted returns than financial stocks. This is based on the history of the Barclays Capital Securities Index versus the S&P 500 Financial Index.

As discussed in chapter 1, part of the evolution of subordinated debt are "CoCos." They are loss-absorbing hybrid securities issued by banks. They present debt obligations that either convert into equity or allow principal to be written down, often at a predefined capital trigger. Once converted or written-down, CoCos are fully absorbing capital, without triggering the bank's default. A trigger may be discretionary at the point of non viability ("PoNV"), or well defined upon the issuance of the bond. The point of non viability is regarded as the time just before an event of default. CoCos can absorb losses either through conversion into equity or through the instrument principal write-down. The trigger can be either "mechanical" or discretionary, with the latter being dependent on the local regulator's judgment. With reference to mechanical triggers, a CoCo can have one or more that are contractually set in the bond terms and conditions, and are usually at a specific Common Equity Tier 1 (CET1) ratio. The loss absorption mechanism is triggered on the breach of that solvency ratio.

Depending on the level of the trigger, CoCos are classified in two different groups:

- High-trigger CoCos (7%–8%) or "going-concern" capital. These instruments recapitalize the banks well before the entity reaches the PoNV. Through conversion/write-down they help restore confidence and stabilize the bank's capitalization at a specific moment in time when a bank suffers from a low-frequency but high-loss event such as a large trading loss. The bank would still be considered to be solvent even without the conversion/write-down, but its capital level would be deemed as modest.
- Low-trigger (around 5%) or "gone concern" capital. Without the conversion/write-down of low-trigger CoCos, the entity would be deemed as insolvent, with the only available alternatives being bankruptcy or recapitalization through state intervention.

The trigger is crucial for the evaluation of the bond as it determines the probability of conversion. That is, needless to say, ceteris paribus, the higher the trigger, the higher the probability of conversion. The loss absorption mechanism of some CoCos can be activated at the PoNV. The PoNV trigger is based on the supervisors' judgment of the issuing bank's solvency prospects. That is, the regulator can impose losses on bondholders if it believes that such action is necessary in order to prevent the issuing bank from becoming insolvent. While the discretion of the PoNV trigger gives authorities great flexibility in managing a crisis situation, it also creates uncertainty for bondholders regarding the performance of their investments. The loss absorption mechanism is another key characteristic. The type of loss absorption mechanism is crucial as it determines the final losses to be assumed in case of conversion.

For this reason, it is key to understand the differences between and the implications of both mechanisms for investors. The principal write-down can be either full or partial. Most of the write-down CoCos have full principal write-down features. However, there are some exceptions. In addition, the principal write-down might be permanent or temporary. In this sense, some CoCos include a write-down/write-up mechanism at the full discretion of the issuer, pro rata with the issuer's other write-down instruments, allowing the investor to recover part of his investment. The conversion into equity has a conversion price that can be based on either 1) preset share price or 2) the market price of the share prior to the trigger being activated. The latter usually includes a floor price for the share, in order to limit the shareholders' dilution. Therefore, in that case the price of conversion will be the higher of the market price and the floor price of the share. CoCos can absorb losses either

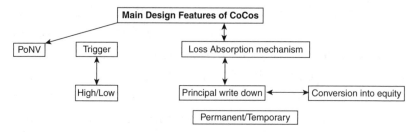

Figure 3.3   CoCo's design diagram.
Source: Author.

through conversion into equity or through the instrument principal write-down. The trigger can be either "mechanical" or discretionary, with the latter being dependent on the local regulator's judgment. With reference to mechanical triggers, a CoCo can have one or more, which are contractually set in the bond terms and conditions, and are usually at a specific CET1 ratio. Figure 3.3 shows the loss absorption mechanism of CoCos.

CoCo debt was issued as a larger effort by the (global) Financial Stability Board (FSB). In November of 2014, the FSB recommended that the largest global banks hold total loss-absorbing capacity (TLAC) of 16 percent to 20 percent of risk-weighted assets (RWAs). TLAC is expressed as a percentage of RWAs and as a percentage of total leverage exposure. In November 2014, it was recommended that global banks have their capital buffer, including the portion coming from the Basel III requirements, at about 20 percent to 30 percent of total capital from the year 2019 onward. CoCos as well as other subordinated debt (Tier 2 or "T2") will be playing a greater role in banks' capital buffers. Therefore, for investors it is relevant to have a grip on what the capital structure of banks will look like going forward. Figure 3.4 on page 125 shows the Basel II and Basel III structure. It is noteworthy that equity will play a larger role in banks' capital.

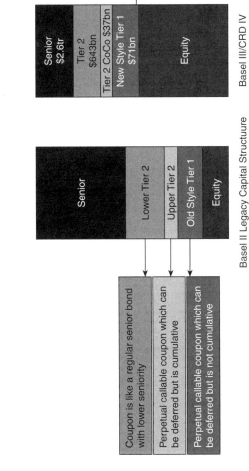

Figure 3.4 Bank Capital Structure in Basel II vs. Basel III.

Source: Basel II, III agreements.

The other significant change is the "New Style Tier 1" debt, known as "AT1." This portion of the capital structure has an equity conversion feature. This feature was implemented to further protect taxpayers in potential future bank bailouts if a government equity injection were required. The AT1 instruments are to absorb losses on a going concern basis, either through a write-down or conversion into equity. This conversion feature has changed the characteristics of the Tier 1 and Tier 2 bonds from the Basel II era.

Tier 1 and Tier 2 financial debt have an equity feature. In that regard, spreads on bank debt often trade with a high beta to equity. Their duration behaves at times like an equity beta. There are several indices developed by Markit, a leading provider of financial information. The company has created CDX indices for sovereign, corporate, and municipal, as well as financial bonds such as CoCos and AT1s. In Figure 3.5, the Iboxx AT1 Euro and Dollar index is plotted against the S&P 500 financials and Eurostoxx financials index. Obviously, there is a strong relationship.

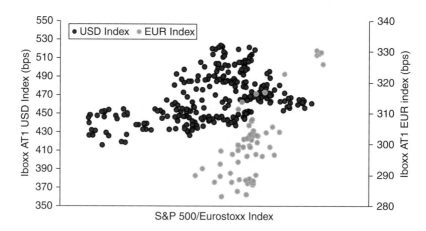

Figure 3.5 Iboxx USD and EUR CoCos/AT1 index vs. S&P 500/Eurostoxx index.

Source: Yahoo Finance, FRB. 2014–2015 daily data.

A regression model has drawbacks because the input variables can have a subjective bias. However, the fact that this model example shows subordinated bonds (or CoCos) are closely related to equities is an important consideration when investing in bank stocks. For investors, too, this means that a long-term, strategic allocation to the global financial sector could be considered primarily in subordinated and contingent convertible bonds. This may act as an alternative strategy to traditional high-yield bonds or equities while enhancing overall portfolio diversification.

Equity-like Debt: Bank Loans, CLOs and ELNs

Bank loans are securities that have a floating rate. The loans are a credit risk, and when interest rates rise, the coupon on the loans rises as well. In a falling rate environment, the coupon on the loans goes down. The maturities of the loans are generally shorter than the maturities of corporate bonds. Banks loans have a callable feature and include amortization and required payments from the cash flows generated in excess. As a result, the average life of bank loans is less than three years. The loans are secured by the company's assets and have a senior position in the capital structure. That is, during a liquidation or bankruptcy, bank loan holders, like the senior debt holders, get the principal protection before the subordinated bond and equity holders.

Collateralized loan obligations (CLOs) are securities backed by a pool of loans or bank debt. The CLO allows the investor to receive scheduled payments from the underlying loans, but the investor also carries the risk in the event the borrowers default. CLOs are sold in tranches that reflect different levels of seniority in the capital structure. CLOs use a high level of leverage, which is on average ten times more assets relative to equity. A CLO operates like a small company in which the managers have access to private pools of capital, generally originating from the bank or insurance sector. Alternatives to CLOs are credit opportunity funds or direct access to loans by individuals or corporations to diversify credit risk. During 2013 and 2014, funds that actively managed bank loans saw their assets grow by 140 billion dollars, which represents about 20 percent of the outstanding loans. Bank loan funds have become popular with the retail audience. To more easily access bank loans, the ETF market may provide opportunity.

According to ETF Database, there are four bank-loan ETFs—all new funds. The biggest one, Power Shares Senior Loan Portfolio, which tracks the S&P/LSTA US Leveraged Loan 100 Index, has more than $6.3 billion in assets, and is only two years old. More than 60 percent of the portfolio is invested in bank loans with credit ratings of B or lower, although its annual dividend yield is 4.46 percent. In Figure 3.6 it is shown that the broad loan index (JP Morgan Liquid Loan Index) is a mirror image of the S&P 500 Index. When distress is high, loans tend to trade like stocks, with yields at record highs, while the stock index saw a plunge

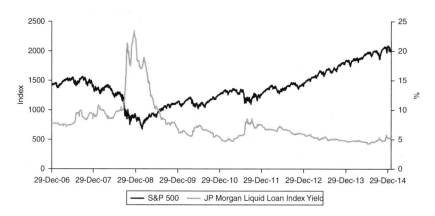

Figure 3.6   Bank Loan Index and the S&P 500 Index.

Source: JP Morgan, FRB. December 2006–2014 *Other Equity like Bonds: Equity Linked Notes.*

during the depth of the crisis from September 2008 through March 2009. Loans, despite their floating rate note features, have risks such as concerns about borrowers' ability to repay their loans.

An equity-linked note (ELN) is structured like a bond, but not like the traditional stand fixed-income security. In an ELN, the final principal payout is linked to the performance of the underlying equity. This can be a single stock or an equity index. ELNs are designed as structured products whereby there is a built-in clause to have principal protection that will return 100 percent of the original investment at maturity. The ELN, however, is different from a standard fixed-coupon bond because the coupon of an ELN is determined by the appreciation of the underlying equity. The ELN is generally structured as a call option on the underlying stock index and a zero-coupon bond. This structure allows for principal protection from the zero coupon bond, and the discount price of that bond to be used to purchase the call option. ELNs do not come without risks like the possibility of default. These three examples (loans, CLOs, and ELNs) are hybrid forms of bonds that can trade like stocks, specifically in times of higher volatility.

Equity and Debt: Going Green

Climate change has climbed to the top of the agenda at almost every gathering of major global leaders, such as the Group or Seven (G7) or Group of Twenty (G20). In recent meetings, the International Monetary Fund (IMF), World Bank, and the World Economic Forum in Davos, climate experts studies have been presented that show there is a need of 700 billion dollars per year to invest in clean and renewable energy, as well as better transportation and limitation to deforestry. The International Energy Agency recommended in its annual report that at least 1 trillion dollars of annual investment is needed to generate a lower carbon world economy. In response to access capital for such massive investments, the United Nations published in 2006 the "Principles for Responsible Investment" (PRI). This report prompted a vast growing base of investors to address environmental, social and governance issues in their guidelines. By 2014, about 1,087 asset owners and investment managers signed up for the principles, representing approximately 45 trillion dollars in assets under management. In addition, about 30 stock exchanges have implemented the requirement to have listed companies disclose their environmental, social and governance practices. The awareness and urgency that something more serious has to be done about the climate has created a vibrant market for green or climate-focused bond and stock investments. The green market is likely to continue to grow as climate change raises the urgency for renewable energy and low carbon industries. Although the green bond market remains in its infancy, the universe in green stocks has expanded more rapidly over the past ten years. Investors who are tempted by green investing need to use caution when selecting green funds. Some of the eco-friendly sectors may experience high volatility, as illustrated by bankruptcy of multiple ethanol and biofuel producers, as well as struggles among small solar power companies, amid the sharp fall in oil prices. It is also important to recognize that investing in companies that have a green focus may not necessarily benefit the environment directly. Green investing has "a less direct impact" on the environment than personally polluting less and recycling. Green investing is a subset of socially responsible investing, in which fund managers and other investors typically use a set of ESG criteria to filter through stocks of companies.

These criteria usually relate to environmental, social and corporate-governance issues.

A wide range of fund strategies with the narrowest funds and ETFs are dedicated to specific sectors, such as solar power or water treatment. Others hold a mix of such stocks, and because they are a little more broadly diversified, their performance tends to be less volatile over time. Less common are funds that consider green factors in their stock selection but also include a broad enough range of stocks to serve as a core holding in an investment portfolio. Most green mutual funds and ETFs are on the smaller side, with all but a few having less than $300 million in assets. A couple of the narrow sector ETFs are among the largest portfolios. There are ETFs that give investors exposure to areas including ethanol, solar and wind power, and energy efficiency. There are others that invest in companies that generally derive 50 percent or more of their revenue from water-related businesses, including water utilities, water treatment companies, and firms that are involved in the infrastructure and distribution of water. Other, more long-standing investment vehicles participate in various areas of alternative energy, including wind, solar, and hydropower, as well as in companies focused on energy efficiency and pollution reduction. Like traditional socially responsible funds, they tend to steer clear of certain sectors, including nuclear power, coal, and oil, and incorporate screens for other social issues. Other mutual funds focus on companies that provide solutions to environmental concerns and those that have environmentally sustainable operations. Examples of companies these funds hold include energy-efficient manufacturer SKF AB in Sweden, Internet giant Google Inc., pharmaceutical company Novartis AG, Toyota, and Honda.

4
Options

Noise is often associated with a rise in volatility. There are two kinds of volatility: the volatility of price and the volatility of value. Fischer Black, an American economist, argued this in his 1986 paper titled "Noise." Markets become imperfect when noise is in control. Without traders reacting to noise, however, trading in assets diminishes and liquidity deteriorates. Some "noise" is therefore needed—albeit not desired. Noise and information are not the same thing, however. When short-term volatility is high and used as input, longer maturity (embedded) options in municipal, corporate, and mortgage bonds tend to be "systematically" overpriced. This maturity mismatch between volatility and value sees over time a convergence, as Black says, because the percentage change in price should eventually fall below the percentage change in value. Specialized traders and fund managers have devoted considerable time and effort to developing derivative models that are calibrated to the market, usually in view of pricing what the "fair" value of volatility should be considering that the world experiences every day a lot of noise. In terms of volatility, a question that should be asked is, what should the implied volatility be if an investor only has information of historical volatility? Classical historical volatility estimation provides one number defined as the annualized standard deviation of log-returns:

$$\sigma_{hist} = \sqrt{\frac{252}{N-1}\left(\sum_{i=1}^{N}\ln\left(S_i/S_{i-1}\right)^2 - \left(\frac{\ln\left(S_N/S_0\right)}{N}\right)^2\right)},$$

where S_i is the spot value of the ith day and $\ln\left(S_n/S_0\right)$ the log returns. An important application of the formula is the arbitrage between implied and historical volatility. Implied volatility is the volatility parameter that needs to be input into the Black-Scholes formula to match the option market price.

Historical volatility measures the fluctuations of the underlying price. When these two volatility values are out of line, then dynamic replication through delta hedging captures some of the difference. Common practice is to compare the at-the-money implied volatility of some maturity with the historical volatility to assess the viability of the arbitrage. Usually, the latter is higher than the former, and the associated strategy is to sell the at-the-money (ATM) option and to hedge it with a delta computed with the implied or the historical volatility. The classical estimate of historical volatility is not representative of the ATM volatility, for at least two reasons. The first one is that it is not linked to a given strike on an option in particular; rather, it is linked to a bundle of strikes over a wide range. The second one is that the standard volatility estimate subtracts the realized drift in volatility, which is not known in advance. This means that historical volatility tends to underestimate the real volatility, which shrinks the usually observed implied to historical volatility ration and puts the volatility arbitrage in question. Indeed, the implied to realized volatility ratio depends on the strike, and it is tempting to run the arbitrage by selling an option of high-implied volatility to attempt to capture a higher implied/historical volatility spread. However, the final profit and loss does not purely depend on the realized volatility, but weights it with the gamma of the option, which is highest around the at the money strike. It is thus important to be able to condition the estimate of the historical volatility on levels that will be reached to properly assess the profitability of the volatility arbitrage strike by strike.

For instance, equity markets tend to exhibit negative skews, which is a concise way of expressing that low strikes (puts) are more expensive than high strikes (calls) in terms of implied volatilities. Strategies based on the standard estimates favor the sale of puts, which are then delta hedged. In a nutshell, this strategy captures the value of the option through its implied volatility and has a cost that is aligned on the historical volatility. The delta hedge is linear in the price at each instant and accompanies up to the value of the option. The hedge ratio (the delta) is computed so as to render the combined position indifferent to an increase or a decrease of the underlying price. Once the delta is hedged, one is left with a second-order term, which is directly linked to the realized (historical) volatility and which is multiplied by the convexity (the gamma) of the option. The gamma depends highly on the option value change that is caused by a change in the delta. The arbitrage between implied and historical volatility consists in capturing the (implied) volatility as contained in the option price and by delta hedging it. The delta hedge has a cost that relies on the historical volatility. It can be seen as swapping daily implied volatility (by collecting time value premium) against the realized return that is driven by the gamma of the option.

The final profit and loss (P&L) hence depends on the quadratic average of the returns weighted by the gamma, which is in essence what the break-even volatilities capture. Option volatilities are generally computed in the Black-Scholes model, which is based on log normal returns. Volatility has met broad acceptance by the trading community, which comfortably manipulates concepts such as the surface of implied volatilities. On some markets, traders have strong opinions on how volatilities should differ across strikes and maturities. On other markets, they are less sure or do not have a good idea because there is too much noise caused by significant headline news. In all cases, it is important to have a method that provides a guideline of what the volatility surface should look like.

One of the challenges when thinking about volatility is how to think about the implied volatility of different strikes. This is known as "skew." Especially for short-dated equity options, such skew is to compensate sellers of downside puts or sellers of upside calls. An investor would want to understand the level of implied volatility where the option strategy breaks even, defined as "breakeven volatility." The idea behind breakeven volatility is that, using only the history of the underlying asset, the "realized skew" can be calculated. When an investor chooses a time period when the stock market fell sharply, the "realized skew" will be quite steep (a large difference between put and call values across different strikes) and implied volatility will be high. Looking over a longer time period and averaging, one can get a sense of realized skew over time.

The concept of breakeven volatility is fairly straightforward. For a given strike and maturity of the option, breakeven volatility is the volatility that should have been used to calculate the value of an option that generates a zero profit. The S&P 500 Index options are a good example of breakeven volatility. If one looks at the breakeven volatility skew by strike (index level) in Table 4.1, the volatility differences between the 1700 index strike and the 2500 index strike are called "skew." In general, skews tend to be higher in the "high volatility period" because the market was falling quickly and delivering high volatility around the low index strikes. This volatility difference is the "implied skew" between low-strike and high-strike options (expressed by column "last" in Table 4.1). The implied skew can be higher than the realized skew (expressed by column "average" in Table 4.1) during high volatility times. Notably, Table 4.1 shows that the difference between the implied and the realized skew for 3-month expiry options is negative (-0.5) the 18-month expiry (+1.2) If an investor has a longer term positive view on the S&P 500, she would choose to (tactically) sell 18-month expiry puts. If an investor has a bearish view, she could choose to sell 3-month expiry calls. There are many different combinations that are possible based on the data in Table 4.1 and the view of the direction of the S&P

Table 4.1 S&P 500 break-even volatility (2009–2014)

Break Even Volatility Data	3M expiry		18M expiry		24M expiry	
Index strike (calls & puts)	Avg	Last	Avg	Last	Avg	Last
1,700.00	11.91	14.33	12.27	12.16	12.28	11.76
1,800.00	11.79	13.96	12.14	11.93	12.17	11.73
1,900.00	11.74	15.07	12.03	11.7	12.07	11.71
2,000.00	12.01	13.83	11.91	11.44	11.99	11.7
2,100.00	11.31	10.68	11.8	11.18	11.88	11.66
2,200.00	9.54	7.8	11.7	11.1	11.76	11.65
2,300.00	8.96	10.33	11.6	11.58	11.62	11.55
2,400.00	9.09	11.16	11.5	11.38	11.46	11.44
2,500.00	8.98	11.92	11.4	10.12	11.31	11.28

Source: Yahoo Finance data 2009–2014. 3mth implied skew is 14.33–11.92 = 2.41 while 3m realized skew is 11.91–8.98 = 2.91. The difference (2.41 – 2.91) is negative, indicative that selling short dated put options is less attractive.

500 Index. This example can be applied to every stock index that has listed options. The realized versus the implied skew is a quick way of assessing whether stock index volatility is cheap or expensive and what is favorable to sell (calls or puts) for what expiry (one to three months or longer).

To put the analysis of Table 4.1 into further perspective, the S&P 500 Index is often associated with a "trailing index put." Especially since 2009, when the Federal Reserve began quantitative easing, S&P 500 companies embarked on share buybacks, and equity index funds gained popularity, the S&P 500 has been in a steady trend upward. Along the way, equity and bond volatility continued to fall, with occasional volatility spikes as a result of smaller, rolling crises such as Europe's debt crisis, the US debt ceiling, Middle East violence, and the Russia-Ukraine conflict. Despite uncertainty that in the past was a catalyst for significant equity underperformance, a covered put strategy on the S&P 500 Index has been highly profitable. That is because, ironically, uncertainty was continuously addressed by monetary policy that drove borrowing costs down so that companies could cheaply finance their share buybacks and pay high dividends to the stockholders. At the same time, uncertainty drove (retail) investors to passive instead of active equity strategies, which is why the equity index funds have seen significant inflows since 2009.

Figure 4.1 on page 141 shows the cumulative return of a rolling long position in the S&P 500 Index futures combined with selling a 3- and 18-month 25-delta (2.5%) out of the money put against the normalized trend of the S&P 500 Index. When taking into account the previous analysis on skew and break-even volatility, selling puts by using the skew analysis may further enhance the return. By positioning in equity index futures and selling options on those futures, there is a leverage component on the underlying futures position. If the short put position gets exercised, the investor would be adding to the existing long futures position. Options and futures require margin, but the position in them is backed by a low amount of capital against significant price return upside potential (or downside potential). A covered put or call position with the position in the underlying index futures in the same direction has more downside than such a strategy when the position in the underlying is in the opposite direction.

There are option strategies that can be applied when the stock benchmark index posts small gains. For example, the Chicago Board of Options Exchange (CBOE's) S&P 500 2% out-of-the-money (OTM) Buy Write Index (BXY), which tracks the performance of monthly 2 percent OTM call sales on the S&P 500, has historically outperformed in periods of low S&P 500 returns. In periods of high returns for the S&P 500, such as during 2009 and 2014, the call writing strategy

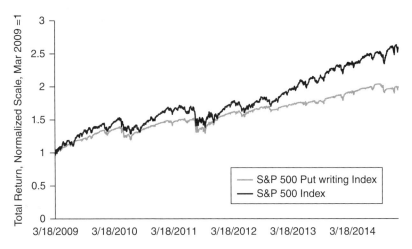

Figure 4.1 SPX Index and put write strategy on the index, cumulative return.

Source: Yahoo Finance, FRB. daily 3/19/2009–12/31/2014. Total Return index, normalized scale, 3/19/2009 = 1.

lagged the S&P index. When S&P 500 returns have been between 0 percent and 5 percent, investors implementing the BXY overwriting strategy would have outperformed the index by an average of 264 basis points (2.64 percentage points). The cost of the BXY strategy has been rolling 0.07 percent monthly. Systematically overwriting a stock portfolio by selling equity index options can generate reasonable return to reduce portfolio risk. During periods of low realized volatility, investors may prefer to increase yield by selling calls that close to being in the money. Income-oriented investors concerned about a Federal Reserve rate hike risk to stocks that have high-dividend yields, may find call writing an appealing alternative "strategy" compared to a buy-and-hold stock. Traders, especially covered call writers, would in this case more favor the "forward roll."

The forward roll strategy helps avoid or defer exercise, creates additional income, and helps keep ownership of stock that is on an uptrend. But there are also risks involved with such a strategy. Rolling forward call options prolongs the exposure to options and can thereby tie up capital. When options are rolled, an investor buys calls to close the original short call position and replaces the old calls with a sell to open, later-expiring new short call position. This means, however, exposure to exercise risk and margin calls for an extended period of time. An investor can question whether rolling calls (or puts) makes sense.

Rolling calls to the same or a higher strike can end up in a loss. By intending to avoid exercise, positions are rolled to a lower strike. The lower strike means a lower capital gain when the call is exercised because it is based on the assumption of a decline in the underlying value in order for the call to work. This may mean a profit in the call may be offset by a smaller capital gain (or a loss) in the underlying upon the time the option is exercised. It makes more sense at times to take a small loss or even to accept an earlier exercise. Given how close the outcomes are in many option rolling instances, and also thinking about the risk coming from extra time exposed to a short position in the option, an investor might be better off buying to close at a loss and waiting out a better covered call situation.

There are some unintended tax consequences with rolling covered call or put option strategies. There are tax rules involved that cover "unqualified" covered calls. There is an alternative by opening a qualified position. When the stock price moves up, an investor should be rolling forward to the same strike and a later expiration date. This option rolling is treated as two separate transactions, and the new option position that has a later expiration date that ends up deep in the money, could be classified as "unqualified." Investors considering this strategy should discuss with their tax professional.

Structural Theta

Options can be a source of income to a portfolio. By buying or selling options, the risk metrics of the portfolio can be dynamically managed. The option positions are sometimes referred to as "synthetic duration" in fixed income portfolio management. A bond portfolio's duration can be synthetically managed by selling options on Treasury note futures. The options are trade on the Chicago Mercantile Exchange and the Chicago Board of Trade. When the options are close to being at the money, they can impact the duration of the portfolio. There are different ways of applying options to a bond portfolio. The strategies fall under the numerator of "structural theta." This strategy is specifically about consistently selling options under the premise that implied volatility is always mean reverting. There are times, however, when volatility rises quickly because there is headline news ("noise") or the options market experience a positioning unwind. The combination of noise and positioning present an opportunity to sell options. That is because when volatility suddenly rises, it causes the option premium to be excessive. An investor could collect this premium by selling options. The excess premium would be well above the premium that constitutes a "fair" level of the options that are priced with volatility that contains less noise. For those reasons, there is a "rich-cheap" analysis for options when the premiums deviate substantially from the underlying value of the asset. A way of potentially enhancing the return of a portfolio is by selling options with a time to expiration of one to three months. The options would be sold against the position in an underlying bond or bond futures contract.

For example, Treasury note futures traded on the Chicago Board of Trade have listed options that are actively quoted. Those options are calls and puts on the ten-year Treasury note future for different strikes and different maturities. Depending on the view of the near-term direction in interest rates, an investor would sell calls or puts against her long position in the Treasury note future. The premium collected from the options can increase the yield on the underlying Treasury future presuming that volatility (and thereby futures price movement) remains range bound and stable. The option premium of the option would then be collected in addition to earning the coupon plus principal and price return. Option selling in an environment in which volatility mean reverts is called a "yield enhancement strategy." Another consideration in selling options is to manage the duration of the portfolio. For simplicity, let us assume the portfolio would only consist of a ten-year Treasury future. The portfolio duration would be about eight years. When selling a call option on the ten-year Treasury future that has an expiration in one month's time, with a strike that is 2.5 percent (called 25-delta) out of the money, the investor accepts that interest rates may rise (selling a call is the same as buying a put). When the price of the Treasury future falls, the collected premium from the call option would cushion the capital loss. At the same time, however, the strike of the call provides an entry point to sell the ten-year Treasury future in order to adjust the duration of the portfolio down as interest rates rise further. Options are therefore a synthetic way of adjusting portfolio risk without changing portfolio composition. In case of a written put, the portfolio manager expects rates to fall and wants to use the option exercise to increase the portfolio's duration. An equity portfolio manager could do the same by buying calls on stable dividend paying stocks and using the exercise to increase the equity duration.

There is a relationship between bonds, stocks, and options. The put-call parity explains that linearly. The relationship between the common stock and the firm can be expressed in terms of options. Stocks can be viewed as a call option on the firm, whereas the cash flow to the stockholders is a function of the cash flow to the firm. The stockholders receive nothing if the firm's cash flows are below the firm's value. In that case, all of the cash flows go to the bondholders. However, the stockholders earn a dollar for every dollar that the firm receives above its (long-term) value. The payoff looks exactly like a call option, with the underlying asset the firm itself. For the bondholders it is the opposite. The cash flow schedule shows they would get the entire cash flow of the firm if the firm generated less cash than its value. Bondholders are entitled only to interest and principal described by two claims as they own the firm and have written a call against the firm with an exercise price of the firm's value.

The stockholders' position, however, can be expressed by three claims. They own the firm, they owe interest and principal to the bondholders, and because of the possibility of debt default, the stockholders have a put on the firm. This put can be viewed from the bondholders' perspective by writing a call option to the stockholders. With a theoretical "riskless default-free" corporate bond, the bondholders are owed principal and interest. The risk of a bond can be expressed in terms of a riskless bond and a put. That is, the value of a riskier bond = value of a "risk-free" bond minus the put option on the firm. In other words, the value of the risky bond is the value of the default-free bond less the value of the stockholders' option to sell the company for its current market value. With the positions of the stockholders and the bondholders viewed either in terms of calls or in terms of puts, the two viewpoints can be expressed as the put-call parity. This parity is generally known as the price of underlying + the price of a put = the price of a call + present value of exercise price. This could be rewritten when expressed as options of shareholders and bondholders:

Value of call on the firm = Value of the firm
+ Value of put on the firm
− Value of risk free bond.

This equation could be applied to a corporation that issued debt and stock. In broad terms, an investor could compare the S&P 500 Index with the Investment Grade Credit Default Swap Index (IG CDX Index). This index is a standardized bilateral over-the-counter derivative contract. The contract transfers the risk of the loss of the face value of a reference basket of debt issuers over a specified period. The CDX spread is determined by two parties: the CDX protection seller who buys "insurance" against credit risk, and the CDX protection buyer who sells insurance to capture credit risk. The basic CDX contract is a "pure" credit risk transfer mechanism, isolating credit risk from interest rate risk, foreign exchange rate risk, and security-specific risk. CDX indices have over the past five years seen an increased correlation with the S&P 500 Index.

A high correlation between the IG CDX and the S&P 500 says that there is a high correlation in volatility. In other words, if the S&P 500 Index were to experience higher volatility, this should translate into volatility in the IG CDX spread. Unfortunately, an active options market on corporate bonds does not exist. What does exist is an options market on the CDS market for investment grade, which is the IG CDX options market. IG CDX option contracts express the right to buy or sell protection on a CDS index, at a particular strike, on a specific future date. The over-the-counter (OTC) contracts trade across a range of strikes and have maturities up to 12 months. CDX and the S&P 500 Index have a close relationship. That is measured by, for example, the correlation in terms of price and volatility. To use the implied volatility of the CDX and the S&P 500, there is a correlation that indicates when investment-grade credit bonds trade more like stocks and when the bonds do not. This relationship between stocks and bonds is the result of "implied correlation." There are changes in the relative premium between index options and single-stock options. A single stock's volatility level is driven by factors that are different from what drives the volatility of an index (which is a basket of stocks). The implied volatility of a single-stock option simply reflects the market's expectation of the future volatility of that stock's price returns. Similarly, the implied volatility of an index option reflects the market's expectation of the future volatility of that index's price returns.

However, index volatility is driven by a combination of two factors: the individual volatilities of index components and the correlation of index component price returns. Intuitively, one would expect that the implied volatility of an index option would rise with a corresponding change in the implied volatilities of options on the index components. Yet, there are times when index option implied volatility moves and there is no corresponding shift in implied volatilities of options on those components. This outcome is due to the market's changing views on correlation. The relationship between the implied volatilities of options on an index and the implied volatilities of a weighted portfolio of options on the components of that index, therefore, becomes a measure of the market's expectation of the future correlation of the index components—the "implied" correlation of the index. When measuring implied correlations of the CDX Index and Treasury note future versus the S&P 500 and the VIX index—CBOE volatility index—Figure 4.2 on page 149 shows there is a reasonable fit between the correlations of each index. The graph says that in periods of high implied correlation between Treasuries and the S&P 500 Index, the implied correlation for the CDX index falls. That suggests the market is trading with more interest rate sensitivity than credit risk sensitivity. This happened during periods when the US economy picked up in growth in late 2010 and the middle of 2013 and that coincided with a potential change of Fed policy toward tightening. This heightened expectations of a change in interest rates, and as a result, the S&P 500 Index traded with greater sensitivity to the prospect of higher rates. In a situation in which the US economy were to weaken, it is possible the implied correlation between the S&P 500 and CDX Index would be high. In that case, the S&P 500 Index would be trading with more sensitivity to the widening in credit spreads that are the result of a pick up in default expectations as the economy worsens.

In other periods, like during the US debt ceiling crisis in 2011, the CDX Index implied correlation to the S&P 500 Index rose, while the Treasury rate implied correlation to the S&P 500 Index fell. Figure 4.2 shows the historical relationship of implied correlations of the CDX Index and Treasury note future to the S&P 500 Index. The 2011 debt ceiling crisis is an example of a situation in which stock market performance is mainly driven by credit risk. The result was that, during the US debt ceiling crisis and subsequent downgrade of the United States by the S&P rating agency, the S&P 500 Index dropped 15 percent, while credit spreads widened. In another episode—the taper tantrum from May to August 2013—credit and interest rate correlations went up together. That is an unusual phenomenon where the market does not differentiate between credit and interest rate risk. During the taper period, Treasury bonds became riskier because of perceptions that the Fed's favorable influence on prices would wane. As a result, other assets reacted negatively because of

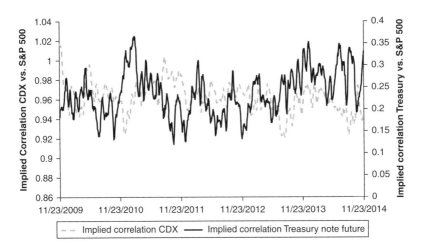

Figure 4.2 Implied correlations equity versus Bonds.

Source: Yahoo Finance, FRB, daily data 2009–2014. Implied correlation CDX = (CDX vol²-VIX²-S&P500 Index vol²)/(2*VIX*S&P500 vol). Implied correlation Treasury Note = (TY vol²-VIX²-S&P500 Index vol²)/(2*VIX*S&P500 vol).

a higher than perceived "risk-free rate." Credit risk premiums had to adjust and that created higher volatility in credit bonds. For cross-over investing, this means that the change in implied correlations can be a sign when bond and stock valuations are closely related and when they are not.

There is a simple strategy an investor can follow without using options on both bonds and stocks. This could be a combination of buying and rolling seven-year Treasuries and by selling 2.5 percent out of the money (25-delta) puts on the S&P 500 Index. This strategy is a long bond and a long stock portfolio. The main macro theme of this portfolio is central bank policies that use asset prices (stocks and bonds) to stage a sustainable economic recovery. An investor may in that environment benefit from both sides of the "central bank trade" consistently. The central bank buys bonds to lower interest rates, so the position in the seven-year Treasury bonds should see continuous price appreciation. If the central bank is relatively successful, the stock market will perform over time. The payoff profile of this strategy looks like the finance theory previously discussed. The strategy of holding a seven year Treasury bond and selling puts on the S&P 500 Index is equal to the value of a call on the stock index plus the value of a "risk-free" bond. Rolling a seven-year Treasury would be a one-year horizon to capture the carry and roll-down return under the assumption that short-term interest rates would remain relatively the same. Rolling puts would also be for a one-year horizon to match the bond investment leg of the portfolio. Figure 4.3 on page 151 shows the cumulative return of a long seven-year Treasury and selling out of the money S&P Index puts and calls portfolio.

This strategy is not without risks, obviously. A seven-year Treasury bond carries a reasonable amount of duration, and selling out of the money puts on the S&P 500 would incrementally increase equity index exposure. That said,

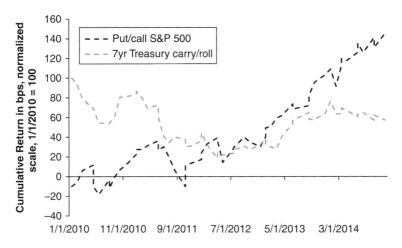

Figure 4.3 Bond-Stock portfolio in options.

Source: Yahoo Finance, FRB, 2010–2014, monthly data. Carry return is expressed in unit of duration and volatility.

this strategy can be expanded by adding corporate bonds or municipal bonds to the mix while selling a (covered) equity index put. And because the era of global central banking in such unconventional territory, a long equity and long government bond portfolio has been advantageous. This portfolio may ultimately change when monetary policy moves in the direction toward a tightening cycle. Then an investor should consider doing just do the opposite: sell 2.5 percent out of the money calls on the S&P Index and roll a short position in Eurodollar futures with a two-year maturity (as a proxy for seven-year Treasuries).

Currency Options

While there is not always a clear-cut way of combining equity and bond options, such can be replicated by currency options. Currency options are generally accessible to individual investors. A type of option available to retail forex traders for currency option trading is the single payment options trading (SPOT) option. SPOT options have a higher premium cost compared to traditional options, but they are easier to set and execute. A currency trader buys a SPOT option by inputting a desired scenario, and a premium is quoted. If the buyer purchases this option, then the SPOT will automatically pay out should the scenario occur. Essentially, the option is automatically converted to cash. Currency options are straightforward to implement when trading straddles, strangles, spreads, or butterflies. When currency options first came on the scene, they were traded over the counter (OTC)—where institutions and broker/dealers trade with each other over the phone to hedge their foreign currency exposure. With institutions dealing with transactions in the billions, this makes sense, especially since, unlike stocks/futures/options, there is no central trading location for foreign exchange. However, many retail online brokerage firms as well as larger institutions provide electronic access to forex liquidity pools that also include the trading of currency options online. Many of the options traded via these firms are still considered OTC as the trader (customer) transacts directly with the broker, rather than matching the order with another trader.

In this case, the broker becomes the counterparty to the currency option and hence has to wear the risk. This also means that currency options can be catered to the individual trader. Without a standardized set of rules dictated by an exchange, a trader can choose the strike/expiry and, in rare cases, the expiration style of the contract that is traded with the broker. Not all electronic trading destinations for currency options are OTC. There are firms that provide liquidity pools for institutions to transact with one another, often called dark pools. For example, HotSpot, FXAllm and CurrenX are all liquidity destinations for the forex market. In addition to forex liquidity pools and OTC with brokers, currency options are also traded on exchanges. For example, the PHLX (NASDAQ) and the Chicago Mercantile Exchange both offer currency options on currency futures. These products will also be accessible by most retail online FX option brokers. FX options are generally European, and hence can use a standard Black-Scholes model. Like an equity option, currency options can be priced using a standard Black-Scholes option model with a dividend yield. With a currency option, the dividend yield represents the foreign currency's continually compounded "risk-free" interest rate. When pricing foreign currency options, the interest rates of both countries need to be considered and entered into an option pricing model—unlike other types of options, such as equity options, futures options that only take one input for interest rates to derive a theoretical price. This interest rate differential between two currencies can be considered as the "cost of carry" for the particular currency spot. Like in bonds, there are equity linked products such as the Equity Linked Foreign Exchange Option (ELF-X). These options are a combination of a currency option and an equity forward contract. When the exchange rate level works in the investor's favor under the option contract, the total payout from the option is dependent upon the performance of the equities index underlying the forward/futures contract. Otherwise, the investor does not receive a payout.

For example, if an investor holds an ELF-X call option on the dollar relative to the Euro, and the Euro currency depreciates relative to the dollar, the investor would not receive a payout. However, if the dollar depreciates relative to the Euro, the investor would receive the amount saved from the use of the spot exchange rate in the option contract and the foreign-equity portfolio value, less the premium paid for the call option. An investor can replicate a bond and equity position in a portfolio through a currency option. The bond is a cash flow of a discounted coupon and a stock is a discounted cash flow of dividend. Together, a bond and stock can be viewed as a swap. The swap represents earning a fixed coupon or stable dividend that is financed with funds borrowed in money markets to purchase the bond or stock. In other words, the investor swaps short-term money market funding for a fixed interest rate (coupon) or dividend. Currencies can also be seen in terms of a swap. The foreign exchange (FX) swap is a simultaneous purchase and sale of identical amounts of one currency for another with two different value dates (spot to forward). Currency options are an option on an FX swap with similar economics.

Why then is an FX swap or an option on an FX swap a replicate of a portfolio of options on bonds and stocks? Consider that a foreign exchange transaction involves two parties that exchange interest rates in a foreign and a home country. In that context, consider the option on a multinational stock that pays a stable dividend and issues corporate debt in a foreign currency. For example, a United States-based investor purchases a call option on a multinational stock that does, for example, most of its business in Europe. The investor also buys the corporate bond denominated in Euro, and subsequently sells a call on the Euro versus the dollar. The entire transaction is a swap facilitated by the FX option. The investor would again use this equation:

Value of call on the firm = Value of the firm
+ Value of put on the firm
− Value of risk free bond,

The value of the firm can be rewritten as value of call − value of put + value of "risk-free" bond. The FX option may play as an "equalizer" between the value of the call stock in local currency and the value of the bond denominated in foreign currency. Like the cross-currency basis swap (chapter 2), the FX option swaps the coupon of the foreign-denominated corporate bond into the domestic currency. In transactional summary, using IBM as an example, here is how such an option strategy would look (using December 2014 values):

- buy 1,000 contracts of the IBM 165 price (25-delta) strike one-year expiry call at 11.5 dollars premium
- sell one-year expiry Euro put/buy USD call 25-delta strike at 1.35 percent premium
- buy IBM five-year Euro-denominated corporate bond at 1.35 percent yield/1.625 percent coupon

The annual cash flow is earning coupon of 1.65 percent plus 1.35 percent collected from the currency option premium equals the premium paid on the IBM call. The investors choose here to be long the IBM capital structure (that is being long both the stock and bond). The bond and stock exposure is hedged for the currency risk for a period of one year. The FX option functions to equalize the one-year fixed return on the IBM stock and bond (all else being equal). Although there are uncertainties or unexpected events during the year, the strategy of using options may provide investors with the flexibility to invest in bonds and stocks of the same company. The majority of options strategies are based on a balancing act between transaction cost, volatility and time value. Most traders want the most time possible so that profits have a chance to develop. They also want to pay the smallest premium possible. As a result, most long strategies require two to three months expiration date at a minimum. An investor can use a variety of spreads to minimize risk and cost, while exposing the position to take advantage when stock prices move in the direction that is expected. An advantage of options is that they are low-cost and flexible instruments. A disadvantage of options is added complexity to the portfolio in terms of unexpected changes in delta or gamma. Without taking actual exposure in the underlying stock or bond, options can replicate such underlying position synthetically. A synthetic long stock position is to by opening a long call position and a short put with the same strike and expiration date. Rather than being long the actual stock, the synthetic option position duplicates the movement in the underlying stock. The difference is that options cost very little or can be structured as a "no cost," that is when the premium of the short option position pays for the premium of the long option. The same synthetic short position in the underlying stock can be replicated by opening a short call and buying a long put that have the same strike and expiration. A position in synthetic short and long options can change in value almost the same as the stock or bond. There are few pros and cons when establishing a synthetic long or short position in a bond or a stock:

1. A synthetic position is a pure replicate of a position in the underlying asset. The risk is the same, but the cost of a synthetic position by using options is very low or even zero. In practicality the option expires, and some synthetic positions can lose more than the principle invested.

2. The short call and long put combination (and vice versa) can nearly entirely hedge the actual long of a short position in the underlying stock. This is specifically the case when the stock market has a clear direction upward (bull market) or downward (bear market). When the market turns south, the long put position increases in value for each point lost in the underlying stock. The maximum loss is the premium paid for the put option. At the same

time, a short option position can provide the same return potential as the underlying asset. The difference is that option positions can be closed or covered or rolled forward to a new expiration date. The underlying asset does not provide all the flexibility that options do. It should be noted that "naked" short options do require 100 percent margin upfront. Risks associated with naked options is unlimited downside because of lack of hedge with the underlying instrument.

Options are very flexible instruments, and they express positions that can be the same as the underlying asset. In a stock and bond portfolio, options play an important role in managing duration and downside risk, while options can add income through premium to the coupon and dividend. Options have "Greeks," such as delta, gamma, theta, vega, and rho. When buying or selling options, an investor has to bear in mind that these variables are the key drivers of an option portfolio. Although options are a contract that is a right or obligation with regard to the underlying asset, option Greeks are complex when the underlying's price or other variables (like interest or dividend) change. The past few chapters provided investors with analysis of how to think about the cross-over idea between stocks and bonds. The final chapter goes into applying the concepts in portfolios.

5
The Portfolio Construction

Adiversified portfolio can be a cash flow stream of income, liquidity and capital. A portfolio is an assembly of securities that should optimally be at the lowest unit of volatility and risk. Portfolio management is mainly concerned with a balancing act to achieve the highest return relative to risk. On the other hand, portfolio management is also concerned with investors objectives and risk tolerance. The next sections focus on methods of securities selection within portfolio construction. In other words, how can fixed income and equity analysis be combined to benefit the asset allocation mix?

Optimal Mix of Stocks and Bonds

Historically, a 60/40 weighted mix of stocks, bonds, and cash produced on average nominal returns of 8.5 percent, with inflation of around 3.5 percent, as seen in Table 5.1 on page 162. The data in the table shows that during different periods, a portfolio with a 60 percent weight in stocks and a 40 percent weight in bonds generally outperformed cash. According to Standard and Poor's research, over the past 15 years, a 60/40 portfolio as presented by the S&P 500 Total Return Index and the Barclays US Aggregate Bond Index had a near 0.98 correlation to the S&P 500 Index. That means a

Table 5.1   Historical returns of 60/40 equity/bond portfolio

Period	Annualized Nominal Returns				
	Equity	Bonds	Cash	60/40	Inflation
1871–2010	8.90%	5.0%	3.70%	7.60%	2.10%
1931–1940	1.80%	4.60%	0.40%	3.90%	–1.30%
1941–1950	12.80%	2%	0.60%	8.60%	5.90%
1961–2010	9.70%	7.40%	5.40%	9.00%	4.10%
1971–1980	8.40%	4.00%	6.90%	6.90%	8.00%
1981–1990	13.90%	14.40%	8.80%	14.30%	4.50%
1991–2000	17.60%	9.40%	4.80%	14.40%	2.70%
2001–2010	1.20%	6.70%	2.20%	3.80%	2.30%
Average	**9.29%**	**6.69%**	**4.10%**	**8.56%**	**3.54%**

Source: Research Affiliates.

portfolio of bonds and stocks would be almost solely determined by the change in the value of the S&P 500 Index. A 60/40 weighted portfolio may be the "benchmark" for an equity/bond mix. There are, however, many variants to "60/40," such as long/short and unconstrained strategies.

Over the past five years, equities and bonds have been key return drivers for investor portfolios by delivering single-digit annualized returns. Briefly after the 2008 crisis, the initial conditions for such a rally were optimal. Earnings multiples were low, asset valuations collapsed, real yields were high, and global central banks embarked on a multiyear easing cycle. In the present environment, equity multiples (PE ratios) have expanded significantly, interest rates are at record lows, and central bank policy has become "divergent." That means some central banks may continue to ease that could be supportive of asset prices, while others may tighten that could be negative. Investors started to question whether a long streak of positive equity and bond returns could continue in the future. Because both asset classes benefitted from post crisis conditions, investors questioned the appropriate weighting of bonds and stocks in their portfolios.

Long/Short and Other Strategies

As a result of changes in perceptions about monetary policy, a range of strategies was exploited such as "long/short," market neutral, traditional long/short, and leveraged long/short. A market-neutral strategy seeks to minimize exposure to the market by balancing long and short exposures. These approaches typically have betas close to zero and seek to deliver modestly positive gains regardless of the market environment. Traditional long/short equity comes in a variety of flavors, and while these are typically long biased, they often offer more flexibility with respect to market exposure. Compared to market neutral and leveraged long/short, traditional long/short seeks more balance between capital appreciation and preservation. Leveraged long/short, which includes strategies commonly known as 130/30, are most similar to long only equity strategy in that they are fully exposed to the market (when the beta of the portfolio equals the beta of the market). Leveraged long/short strategies seek to outperform the market through stock selection in their long and short portfolios. Given these different objectives, there are clear differences in performance during the extreme markets of 2008, when the S&P 500 declined 37 percent, and in 2013, when the market rose 32 percent shown, in Figure 5.1 on page 164.

Adding a comparison of long-term returns and volatility, there are a few conclusions to draw. First, market-neutral strategies tend to better deliver on protecting downside risk mitigation and have generally lower volatility. These strategies may fulfill an important role in an overall portfolio, but they can also serve to diversify away from solely

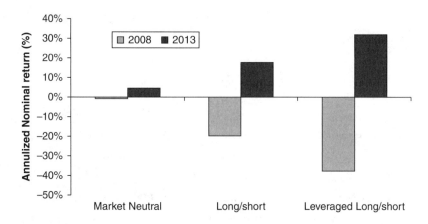

Figure 5.1 Different equity strategies.
Source: Research Affiliates, 2008 and 2013 calendar year.

equity exposure. Therefore, they may be unsuitable for investors who only look to invest in stocks. Second, leveraged long/short and 130/30 strategies have at times delivered attractive returns. As a group, however, these strategies have underperformed the broader market and generally have higher volatility. A long only equity portfolio with an allocation to cash and fixed income may be a better strategy altogether. A long/short strategy has produced the highest risk-adjusted returns of the three strategy types, with equity-like returns and significantly less volatility than equities. This category has generally delivered on the objective of participating in equity market return opportunities while mitigating downside risk.

In the universe of funds, open-ended funds like mutual funds have several advantages to investors. These advantages are liquidity, transparency on what the mutual fund holds, and a fee charged that is fixed. Mutual funds fall under the 1940 Act. This Act applies to companies or entities that trade and invest securities or offer those securities to the public. Mutual funds invest in stocks, bonds, and commodities, but also currencies. As the evolution of the mutual fund complex continued, new versions of the original mutual funds were introduced such as "long/short" mutual fund. These funds offer a limited form of leverage by segregating assets. That means that options and futures positions in the fund have to be covered by liquid assets in the fund. The rule caps the leverage at 200 percent of gross notional exposure by the fund. The "limited leverage" does provide flexibility to the investor who seeks equity exposure but with lower volatility than investing in a single stock or in a private fund that may tie up capital in illiquid securities.

Risks and Variance

An investor can use long/short mutual funds in her portfolio in several ways. A long/short mutual fund serves as a complement to a long-only equity fund. They can be a liquid alternative to single stock positions, and offer in general diversification by investing in a broader portfolio of securities than a typical investor can achieve. Lastly, long/short mutual funds may mitigate overall volatility in a portfolio, thereby further enhancing the benefit of diversification. A crucial lesson of the past ten years is that volatility is the nemesis of wealth accumulation. Since 2009, when the era of quantitative easing began, investors have accrued large gains during an extended (and unusual) period of equity and bond market outperformance. The outperformance, however, has obscured the negative impact of volatility on compound returns. The following equation expresses the relationship between wealth accumulation and volatility:

$$\text{Compound Returns} \approx \sqrt{\text{AvgRet2} - \text{Var(Ret)}}$$
AvgRet = average monthly return to the portfolio
Var(Ret) = variance (or volatility) of monthly returns.

This formula has two important implications:

- If two portfolios have the same average returns, the lower volatility portfolio accumulates more wealth.
- The higher the variance, the more compound returns will lag average returns.

The formula states that investors do not realize the average return of a particular investment over time, but the compounded result of that stream of returns. The average returns and compound returns each have a level of volatility. In finance, the absolute difference between average and compound returns produces volatility. When time progresses and the level of volatility moderates, the compound return improves in risk-adjusted terms versus the average returns that have higher volatility. The volatility of the asset obviously matters, and a careful selection process, that is, picking, is critical. An example of allowing large volatility to enter portfolios was in 2007, when there was a "mad rush" into stocks due to a large volume of leveraged buyouts (LBO) and mergers and acquisitions. At some point, media commentators argued that the entire S&P 500 Index could face the prospect of an LBO. The amount of leverage that entered the financial system, in combination with a peak in imprudent mortgage lending, led to a financial meltdown in 2008. The result was a significant downward adjustment of US equities in portfolios by diversifying into emerging markets and commodities. Figure 5.2 on page 167 shows that from January 2009 through September 2014, all of those decisions would have resulted in lower risk-adjusted performance compared to an investment that remained in a diversified US large-cap stock allocation (Russel 1000).

The preceding analysis shows that under different equity/ bond weights, diversification can be achieved by running

	Annualized Return	Standard Deviation	Annualized sharp ratio
Russel 1000 Index	17.55	15.28	1.13
70%-20%-10% US/non-US/EM	15.8	16.03	0.99
70%-30% US/non-US	15.47	15.94	0.98
80%-20% US/Commodities	14.15	15.07	0.95
MSCI Emerging Index	13.22	21.67	0.68
MSCI EAFI Index	10.47	18.76	0.62
Ishares S&P GSCI Commodity-Index	1.67	18.69	0.18

Figure 5.2   Large-cap equity and diversifying strategies

Source: Research Affiliates, monthly data, 2009–2014.

active or passive strategies. Appropriately weighting a portfolio means active portfolio management because the portfolio weights need to be dynamically adjusted. Nowadays passive strategies have become increasingly popular in equity and fixed income. A passive strategy can also be dynamically weighted, or there can be a combination of passive and active strategies that is dynamically weighted. It is important to note that portfolios today have a "problem", which is home market bias. Think of this as putting all your eggs in one basket: with home-market bias, US investors risk severely limit their income potential because of a large investment opportunity set outside the United States. Constructing a bond and equity portfolio with a home market bias shifts the focus from being diversified across sectors and overweighting securities in a narrowly defined group. This increases concentration risk in the portfolio and the potential for loss if one sector falls in value. A cross-over strategy may help diversify concentration risk, with a caveat that such a strategy has several micro elements. That means that cross-over opportunities between stocks and bonds may not necessarily always perfectly diversify risk.

That said, a cross-over strategy between stocks and bonds can enhance returns with a limited amount of additional volatility. In the following sections, two portfolio strategies are discussed. The first one is a dividend strategy whereby "equity and bond carry" is central. The second strategy is a passive equity index portfolio combined with an active corporate and Treasury bond strategy. *It is important to note that the author has no position in the companies at the time of writing this book. The analysis is not intended and should not be viewed as investment advice to sell or purchase shares or securities of the specific companies discussed.*

Dividend, Coupon and Carry

When companies have high earnings growth, and they pay dividends, investors have been led to believe that they must ask for either dividends or growth, but cannot expect both. That actually means shareholders do not routinely demand a healthy dividend payout from all their companies. US equity sectors most commonly targeted by investors for dividend income are telecoms, utilities, Real Estate Investment Trust (REITs), and Master Limited Partnership (MLPs). These companies also issue senior unsecured and subordinated debt. An investor who wants growth and dividend would also like the companies' bonds to perform. After all, if the default risk on corporate debt goes up, the equity risk is likely to go up too and that would jeopardize earnings and dividend payout. If companies have a stable dividend payout over a long period of time, that should also result in stable returns on their corporate debt. There are different cases to look at to confirm or challenge this. Starting with AT&T, it has steadily paid dividend since the late 1980s. The company has also issued debt since the 2000s that is generally five years in maturity or longer, and mostly

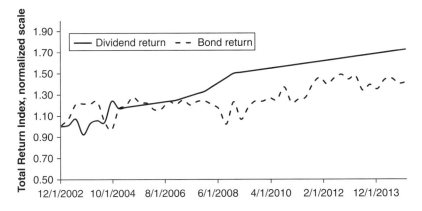

Figure 5.3   AT&T dividend versus bond return.

Source: Yahoo Finance, FRBNY. Monthly data, 2002–2014. Bond return = price return indexed to 12/1/2002 = 1.

has fixed coupons. When one invests in regular dividend-paying stocks, adding exposure in corporate debt means the portfolio reflects the entire capital structure. The AT&T example, shown in Figure 5.3, shows the history of its dividend total return and the corporate bond total return. The bond used is the AT&T 6.5 percent coupon maturing on March 15, 2029. The example of AT&T's earning a dividend of 2 percent and a coupon of 6.5 percent is not necessarily a stable return. Figure 5.3 shows that although the return from dividend was consistent throughout time, the return on the AT&T bond had more volatility.

There is another way of comparing the bond and dividend by looking at "carry." The earlier discussion in chapter 2 on equity carry expressed carry return as a unit of equity duration. When compared to the carry return on bonds, the important assumption is the funding rate. A company, unlike a bank, cannot borrow at the Federal Reserve window. If a company could, then its short-term funding rate would be close to the Federal Funds Rate. In some cases when a company has a high rating (A or better), commercial paper

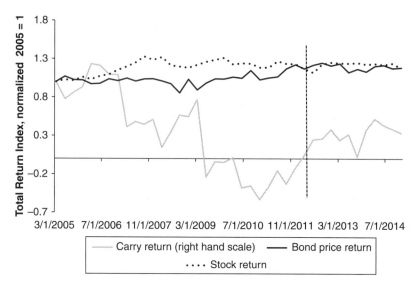

Figure 5.4   Total return indices for AT&T carry, bond, and stock.

Source: Yahoo Finance, FRB. Monthly data, 2005–2015. Carry return = (Dividend yield –
yield of AT&T bond maturing in July 2015)/equity duration + (coupon of T 2029– yield
of AT&T bond of July 2015)/bond duration. Equity duration = 1/dividend yield.

(typically three months' maturity up to one year) is issued
at a small spread to the Fed Funds rate. In most cases, however, investors have to look at short maturity issued debt
for an indication of a company's short term funding rate.
AT&T in this case has issued short-term bonds dating back
as far as 1993. For example AT&T 7 percent coupon maturing in July 2015 could be a historical proxy for short-term
funding. By using the yield of that bond, historically the
equity carry and bond carry per unit of risk can be calculated. When plotting in Figure 5.4 the carry as a total return
index and comparing that series with the total return of the
2029 bond and AT&T's common stock, there is a relationship to note.

The return on AT&T stock and bond started to track
closely when the carry return turned positive by 2012. This
may be the result of falling short- and long-term interest

rates. It can also be caused by the stability of the dividend, which helps improve perceptions of the company and thereby the market rewards AT&T with lower borrowing cost. The lower borrowing cost could improve the carry return and thereby provide stability of the stock and bond total return. The AT&T example shows there is a case for looking at the carry return of a company's stock and bond, and comparing that with the actual returns. It is important to note that the dividend payout and the rating on the debt remain stable. This carry-and-return framework can also be applied in a broader portfolio opportunity set. For the simulation, a selection is taken of regularly paying dividend stocks that have a dividend yield of 2 percent or higher and those companies issue frequently bonds. The results are shown in Table 5.2 on page 172. The companies listed are a REITs, banks, telecoms, consumer discretion, and utility stocks. The Table 5.2 includes the equity and bond carry per unit of duration risk. Stocks and bonds with high and low carry are selected to identify whether carry matters in determining the high and low individual stock performers.

The total return analysis for the group of companies is shown with the results in Figure 5.5 on page 173. The average Sharpe ratio is 0.4 for banks to about 1.1 for utilities. The utility sector is the best performer, and that may be the result of the highest carry per unit of risk, which seems also the most stable in terms of volatility. Banks have lagged the most, in part as they generally offered little additional carry return versus the other sectors. What Figure 5.5 shows is that the correlation between the return indices is high. In other words, the indices have a high beta to the broad market that makes it somewhat questionable what diversification benefits there are to be gained.

Table 5.2 Stock and bond selection

Company	Coupon	Dvd Yld	Debt maturity	Stock duration	Equity carry/dur (bps)	Bond carry/ dur (bps)
ENBRIDGE ENERGY	6.1	5.5	11.9	18.3	10.8	21.9
AT&T INC	4.3	5.4	13.3	18.4	10.5	5.9
VERIZON COMMUNIC	4.8	4.5	14.9	22.4	4.4	8.8
SOUTHERN CO	4.2	4.0	15.4	24.9	2.0	4.6
CHEVRON CORP	2.5	3.9	7.1	25.9	1.4	−13.6
GENERAL ELECTRIC	4.2	3.7	9.0	27.1	0.7	8.1
DUKE ENERGY CORP	4.9	3.6	12.9	28.0	0.2	10.6
DOW CHEMICAL CO	5.4	3.2	12.2	30.9	−0.9	15.9
PG&E CORP	5.1	3.1	16.4	31.9	−1.2	9.6
PFIZER INC	5.0	3.1	9.6	32.2	−1.2	16.1
DOMINION RES/VA	4.5	3.0	16.0	33.2	−1.5	6.1
EXXON MOBIL CORP	3.6	2.9	8.5	34.6	−1.8	0.7
JPMORGAN CHASE	4.1	2.8	7.5	35.4	−1.9	7.9
IBM	3.2	2.8	6.7	35.7	−2.0	−4.1
COCA-COLA CO/THE	2.8	2.8	6.1	36.1	−2.0	−10.6
PROCTER & GAMBLE	3.8	2.7	8.7	36.4	−2.1	3.4
WEYERHAEUSER CO	7.1	2.7	11.5	37.4	−2.2	31.5
GENERAL MOTORS C	4.2	2.7	9.7	37.5	−2.2	6.8
CAMPBELL SOUP CO	4.1	2.6	9.5	37.7	−2.3	5.8
INVESCO LTD	4.0	2.6	13.7	37.9	−2.3	3.8
WELLS FARGO & CO	3.8	2.6	9.0	38.7	−2.4	3.4
PEPSICO INC	3.7	2.5	8.1	39.8	−2.5	2.6
INTEL CORP	2.9	2.5	13.8	40.0	−2.5	−4.3
TARGET CORP	5.0	2.4	11.8	40.9	−2.6	12.3
DEERE & CO	2.8	2.4	5.0	41.0	−2.6	−14.7
SEMPRA ENERGY	4.9	2.3	13.3	43.6	−2.8	10.7
US BANCORP	2.6	2.3	5.4	43.6	−2.8	−16.4
CATERPILLAR INC	3.4	2.3	7.4	44.2	−2.8	−0.7
TEXAS INSTRUMENT	2.2	2.2	3.1	44.8	−2.8	−44.2
ESSEX PROPERTY	4.2	2.2	7.0	44.9	−2.8	9.8
NORFOLK SOUTHERN	5.5	2.1	23.8	47.8	−2.9	8.5
EDISON INTL	4.5	2.1	17.2	48.7	−3.0	6.0

Source: SEC, FRB. Equity carry/unit of duration = Dividend yield − average funding rate/ (1/dividend yield). Carry is quarterly annualized.

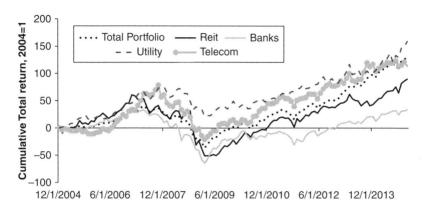

Figure 5.5   Total return indices.

Source: Yahoo Finance, FRB, monthly data December 2004–December 2014, normalized scale. Total return indices of stock prices of the different sectors shown in table 5.6. Series are normalized since 12/1/2004 with equal weights for stocks in each sector.

Carry Portfolios

To address diversification, the analysis is extended by selecting stocks with only positive carry and only negative carry. It should be noted that stocks that have a positive carry are companies that also issue bonds. Those bonds can have a yield that is below or above the dividend yield of the stock. The positive or negative stock carry measures the difference between the dividend and the average short-term funding rate of companies. In the sample case, positive carry stocks are Enbridge, Verizon, GE, Duke, and Southern Corp. The negative carry stocks are Texas Instruments, Deere, Target, Intel, and Coke. The total return analysis in Figure 5.6 on page 174 "disregards" fundamental stock analysis, earnings assessment, and traditional valuation. The stock carry per unit of equity risk is the only dominant factor. What stands out in Figure 5.6 is that an equally weighted portfolio of positive and negative carry stocks can outperform the broader index. Fundamental equity valuation may have resulted in different portfolio weights and constituents. There may be a

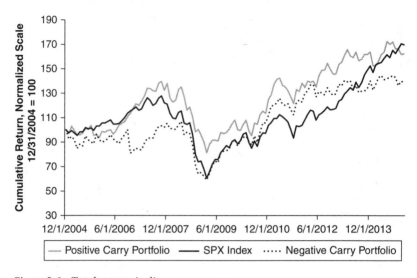

Figure 5.6   Total return indices.

Source: Yahoo Finance, FRB. Monthly data 12/2004–12/2014. The positive carry stocks are Enbridge, Verizon, GE, Duke, and Southern Corp. The negative carry stocks are Texas Instruments, Deere, Target, Intel and Coke. The weights are 20% per stock.

level of "coincidence." The selected stocks happened to outperform the broader index during a time in which the S&P 500 Index beat active managed equity funds. "Carry return" may have been superior because this was an era in which the yield curve was upward sloping, interest rates continued to fall, and interest rate volatility was generally low. Stocks that have stable dividend yields and experience a steady decline in their capital markets funding rate because of a falling rate environment, may have proved to be proper diversification in a stock portfolio. There is obviously no guarantee a stock carry portfolio may result in high returns in the future. Investors should look closely at a company's capital structure and fundamentals like free cash flow and PE ratios. When calculating the average cost of funding and identifying high and low to negative carry stocks, that criterion could be a complement to the fundamental analysis of earnings and free cash flow. Often companies that have a high free cash flow are well capitalized and pay regular high dividend. If they have a weighted average funding rate that remains stable, the carry return (per unit of equity duration) is likely high.

"Passive" Equity, Active Bonds

Since 2009, the popularity of passive index funds and exchange trade funds has grown exponentially. At the same time, the inflow into active bond funds has been equally impressive. After the financial crisis of 2008, investors may have been seeking the best guaranteed "stability" and avoiding financial engineering and creativity. This makes perfectly sense in an environment of deleveraging in which debt is paid down by saving a greater proportion of income. While income is stagnant and uncertain, and credit less available, the additional income had to come from investing in securities. With the excessive losses and volatility in mind from the September 2008 to March 2009 episode, investors sought out stable income sources to supplement their stagnant wages. This may explain why passive equity and fixed-income funds remained in favor despite lower yields and higher equity prices. The conservative strategy could be as simple as investing 50 percent of your cash by buying a seven-year maturity Treasury bond and investing 50 percent in the S&P 500 Index ETF. As discussed in chapter 4, such a Treasury-Equity Index strategy is by holding a seven-year Treasury that would generate a return from carry and roll down (rolling down the curve). The S&P put/call strategy of buying calls and selling puts would generate "theta," accumulative premiums collected from options. Together this strategy is again shown in Figure 5.7 on page 176.

This bond-stock strategy may offer a stable stream of cash flow, provided the yield curve slope does not change all too much and volatility remains low. Many income strategies emphasize stable income because that is what everyone desires. Unfortunately, investing in stocks and bonds is not

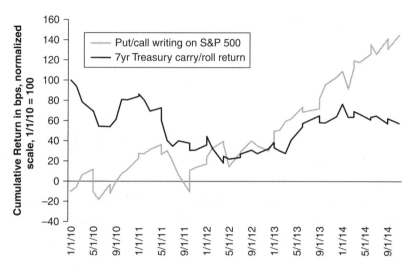

Figure 5.7   Carry and roll strategy.
Source: Yahoo Finance, FRB. Daily data, 2010–2014. Carry is 3mths annualized. The carry return is expressed per unit of duration or volatility (in case of S&P options).

always stable. It requires regular rebalancing to improve the overall return, with investors bearing in mind that higher turnover can increase transaction cost. Investors may choose a passive strategy to avoid those costs. Although a passive strategy is a replication of an index, the index consists of individual securities and companies. In an indirect way, investors are subjected to security selection in a passive strategy because they choose a particular index over other indices that have different constituents. A "passive" investor may not realize such is the case and should therefore consider actively managed index strategies. Security selection, therefore, also plays an important role in passive strategies.

Picking the Right Securities

In an active strategy, the right security "picks" are critical. Investors often use an active strategy to complement their passive strategy. An active strategy versus an index is also about market weights of the portfolio versus the index. There is currently a new generation of indices that has moved some from traditional market capitalization-based indices to alternative strategies, known as "smart beta." The smart beta strategy does not use conventional market weights but rather alternative weights like volatility or dividend. A smart beta strategy is designed as a "passive" strategy by following an index, but adjusts portfolio weights when inefficiencies appear in the marketplace. Successfully applying smart beta strategies can generate similar returns like those in real estate or infrastructure. In any passive or active strategy, however, smart beta is equally subjected to the art of securities selection. In this example, a passive equity strategy and an active bond strategy are combined. It is imperative, however, to apply the bond and stock picking methods together. First, a portfolio of high-quality bonds that consists of corporate bonds, financials bonds, and intermediate to long Treasuries, and longer maturity Treasury Inflation Protected Securities is selected. The stock selection consists out high-quality US stocks that have positive carry and have longer maturity corporate bonds outstanding. To note is that purchasing long maturity credit bonds presents several challenges. First, the holding period is much longer than that for intermediate or shorter maturity bonds. Second, transaction costs as a percentage of annual carry can be meaningfully higher. Finally, liquidity decreases over time as on-the-run 30-year corporate bonds become off-the-run bonds as corporations issue new 30-year bonds. Given these unique challenges, passive investing in long credit does come with higher risks.

Portfolio Construction Approach

When selecting individual stocks and bonds, the process has to be combined with a rigorous top-down macroeconomic-analysis. The macro analysis is to help support views on bond duration and credit sectors. The selection of credit sectors is

conducted by thorough bottom-up credit research to identify companies with sound fundamentals. Selection criteria
are companies and sectors with potential for strong secular
and cyclical earnings growth, aggressive pricing power, have
high barriers to entry and, most importantly, expectations
for deleveraging on a forward-looking basis. Some of the
sectors that look attractive based on these criteria include
utilities, health care, building materials, midstream energy,
pipelines, airlines, retail, and cable. The question is, why
pick these companies and those specific bonds?

A summary from chapter 2 on the basic principles of bond
picking is by looking at these selection criteria:

1) Yield curve: bonds with the highest carry and roll down
   are the "sweet spot" on the curve.
2) Basis: bonds trade with a negative "basis" or to CDS.
3) Financing: bonds can trade special on repo to lend the security at a very favorable, low, or even negative financing rate.
4) A "spline curve": the difference between the actual and
   spline curve identifies "rich" or "cheap" bonds.
5) Butterfly spread: this indicates whether short and long
   maturity bonds trade at a lower or higher yield historically relative to an intermediate maturity bond.
6) On the run: the spread between on-the-run and off-the-
   run bonds measures liquidity premium.
7) Inventory: positions are either proprietary positions or
   leftover positions from a recent new issue that may offer
   attractive pricing versus the secondary market.

A Treasury and Treasury Inflation-Protected Securities (Tips) Portfolio

The valuation methods for Treasury and Tips can be quite
sophisticated. For example, deriving Treasury bond valuation
from the "spline curve," which is a theoretical yield curve by

bootstrapping zero coupon bonds over a timeframe of 30 years. An easier, more straightforward approach is to analyze the Treasury and Tips yield curve today and compare that with their forward curve, which shows expectations of nominal and real interest rates in the future. The difference between today's Treasury and Tips yield curve and the curve five years from today is called "expected inflation." In Figure 5.8, the Treasury and Tips yield curve and expected inflation are shown. If the forward curve of both Tips and Treasury were to be materialized, the returns on all maturities would be negative.

Inflation, however, is expected to remain below the Fed's 2 percent target for the next decade. If that is correct, longer maturity Treasury bonds may have some "value." The reason is that the expected return after adjusting for inflation is moderately positive at around 2 percent to 3 percent (expected inflation plus the real Tips yield five years forward). Some other investors would take an opposing view and would argue that, based on a benign outlook for inflation far into future, short-term interest rates should stay low. If that is

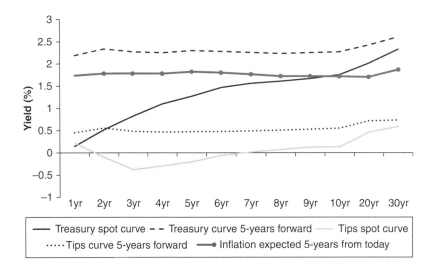

Figure 5.8   Treasury, Tips, and inflation.

Source: Treasury Direct, FRB. Data as of January 2015.

the case, the yield curve may stay upward sloping and that makes intermediate (five- to ten-year maturity) Treasuries and Tips more attractive for investors to buy and hold. One "obvious" reason is that the carry return from intermediate Treasuries is higher because the slope of the yield is the steepest around the five- to ten-year point. Based on the forward curve projection on expected inflation, the expected return in real terms (i.e., adjusted for inflation) on intermediate Treasuries is lower. There is a trade-off to holding Treasury bonds in terms of whether a higher return today or a higher expected return in the future is more important. The portfolio analysis presented here chooses the expected long-term returns because of the future prospects of advanced demographics and excess savings, demand for longer maturity Treasury bonds may remain relatively high.

Corporate Bond Portfolio

The second part of the bond portfolio consists of corporate bonds. The corporate bond universe has about 7.5 trillion USD debt outstanding, according to the Securities Industry and Financial Markets Association (SIFMA, www.sifma.org). There are many bonds to choose from, and for the analysis, the focus is on longer maturity corporate bonds from some of the sectors such as Retail, Utilities, Railroads, Financials, and Healthcare. These sectors are a "fair" representation of the S&P 500 Index. By sector, a large company is chosen. In utilities, there is American Electric Power (AEP) Company. The company specializes in delivering electricity, and has over five million customers in 11 states across the Midwest and Southwest of the United States. The other bonds selected are from Amazon (retail), Verizon (TMT), Union Pacific (Railroads), and Amgen (Healthcare). A selection of financial metrics of these companies are shown in Table 5.3 on page 181.

Table 5.3 Credit metrics for Utilities

(FY 2015)	American Electric	Verizon	Amazon	Union Pacific	Amgen	JP Morgan
Free Cash flow ($, mln)	479	16,647	1,770	2,858	7,037	28,620
Liquidity ($, mln)	2,835	13,756	8,883	3,286	29,526	1,300
Net Debt ot EV	1.5x	2.2x	0.2x	0.3x	1.2x	1.1x
EBITDA/Interest	6x	9.7x	37.9x	19.9x	9.5x	9.5x
Long maturity Corporate Bond	6.625% 11/2037	4.15% 3/2024	4.90% 1/ 2044	4.85% 6/ 2044	5.5% 11/ 2041	4.85% 2/ 2044
Rating	Baa1/BBB	Baa1/BBB+	Baa1/AA–	A3/A	Baa1/A	A3/A
CDS basis/liquidity (bid/ask)	–33bps/ 3–6bps	–25bps/ 3–6bps	–35bps/ 3–7bps	–37bps/ 3–7bps	–33bps/ 3–6bps	–50bps/ 3–5bps

Source: SEC, Company earnings statements as of Q4 2014. EBITDA = Earnings before interest, taxes and depreciation.

AEP is leveraged, but is highly diversified in operations that are expected to deliver 85 percent to consolidated earnings and free cash flow. Their outstanding debt consists mostly of long maturity corporate bonds. Amazon (retail), Verizon (TMT), Union Pacific (Railroads), and Amgen (Healthcare) are companies that have low leverage.

The Equity Portfolio

The other part of the securities selection are the stocks of the companies, shown above in Table 5.3. Unlike the analysis for bonds, stock picking has a different set metrics to determine valuation:

1) Share price should be no more than two-thirds of its intrinsic value.
2) Look at companies with PE ratios at the lowest 10 percent of all equity securities in their peer group.
3) Stock price should be no more than tangible book value.
4) Debt-to-equity ratio is preferably below 100.
5) Current assets should be two times current liabilities.
6) Dividend yield should be at least two-thirds of the long-term government bond yield.
7) Earnings growth should be at least 7 percent per annum compounded over the last ten years.

Based on some of these metrics, Table 5.4 on page 183 summarizes the equity valuation for each of the companies. The PE and PB multiples (except for Amazon) are low, with dividend yields clustered around 2.5 percent to 4 percent.

The Ladder

The bond- and stock-picking criteria that resulted in the securities selection have a few additional points. The bonds were picked for their liquidity profile. Corporate bonds

Table 5.4 Equity summary

(FY 2015)	American Electric	Verizon	Amazon	Union Pacific	Amgen	JP Morgan
P/E	18	13	101	20	16	9
Price to Book	2	15	14	5	5	1
Price to Free cash flow	81	14	85	34.50	15.90	310.00
EV/Sales	2.9x	2.3x	1.85x	4.7x	5.6x	
Dividend yield	3.20%	4.70%	0%	1.63%	2.60%	2.91%
Return on invested capital	6%	32%	3%	18.90%	9.30%	3.50%
Cost of equity	4.40%	5%	9%	9.20%	7.50%	2.60%
10-year annualized equity return	33%	30%	25%	34%	–11%	2%
Current share price	62.8	45.7	354	117.21	152.7	54.3
Divided ex-date/div. amount (cts)	5/8/2015/50cts	4/8/2015/0.55cts		2/27/15/0.5cts	5/12/15/0.65	4/3/15/0.40

Source: SEC, Company earnings statements as of Q4 2014. Share price level as of January 2015. EV = enterprise value, P/E = Price to Earnings.

trade on electronic platforms, but those tend to be accessible to institutions (Market Access, for example). The yield curve in corporate bonds can be upward sloping, but it is more appropriate to look at the "credit spread curve." This is the maturity term structure of OAS spreads. Normally, the OAS spread curve is relatively flat because capital markets demand risk premium for a company based upon long-term rating and short-term liquidity profile. During recent years, because short-term interest rates have been near zero, the credit spread curves have become steeper, whereby longer maturity corporate bonds offer greater risk premium. The corporate bonds in this specific example are "on-the-run" bonds. On-the-run bonds are either tapped by increasing the issue size or are issued with a fair amount outstanding (larger than $1 billion notional). The transaction cost of switching the bonds to other bonds would be relatively manageable. The relative valuation is relevant, but sometimes it can be the "value of the day" measure. Therefore, the bonds were selected on the basis of companies' long-term growth prospects. The distribution of coupons and maturities was also taken into account. Based on maturities starting in March 2024 and ending in June 2044, the cash flow schedule is monthly payments of coupons that are at an average of 5.1 percent. Stacked upon the coupons are the quarterly dividend payments with an average of 50 cents per share (except for Amazon, which does not declare dividend). It is noteworthy that, unlike in fixed income in which a ladder is stable because of fixed coupons, stocks ladder can only work when there is stability of dividend payouts. The selected companies have a good history of stable dividend payouts and no bond defaults. To visualize the ladder, think about a reinvested same amount every year in the same bonds but each time at a different maturity.

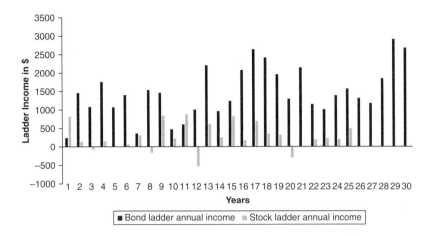

Figure 5.9 Bond and stock ladder.

Source: Author. The ladder measures an investment in six bonds and six stocks for $1,000 each that get consistently reinvested over the life of the security.

For stocks, this could the same strategy, provided the dividend yield remains roughly the same. Under these assumptions Figure 5.9 shows the bond and stock ladder, assuming a 5.1 percent coupon, a 3.5 percent dividend yield, and a 25–30-year maturity.

All Portfolios Combined

Bringing the stock and bond selection together, the focus moves to the portfolio's total return. The portfolio consists out of two Treasury bonds, six corporate bonds, and six stocks of the same companies (for a total of 14 securities). This is the active part of the portfolio, as compared to the S&P 500 Index, which represents the "passive strategy." The combined strategy is then enhanced by looking at changing the constituents of the portfolio with competitor peer companies that may be trading cheaper with their stocks or bonds relative to the current selected group of companies (Amazon, JP Morgan, Verizon, American Electric, Union

Pacific, Amgen). The portfolio has the bonds and stocks at 50/50 percent and 60/40 percent weights. The period of historical performance used is ten years (from 2005 to 2015). The return of the individual securities is measured as the monthly percentage change in price, that is, the price return that includes reinvestment of dividend or coupon interest. The S&P 500 is also measured on its monthly price return, including dividend reinvestment. In this example, the cumulative return of the 50/50 weighted (50 percent in individual stocks and 50 percent in bonds) portfolio is 79 percent with a standard deviation of 27 percent. The 60/40 weighted portfolio has a cumulative 89 percent return with a standard deviation of 30 percent. The S&P 500 cumulative return since December 2005 was 66 percent, with a standard deviation of 24 percent. The results compared show that the individual portfolios have a high correlation to the S&P Index. The information ratios are also quite high. The information ratio is a ratio of portfolio returns above the returns of the S&P Index to the volatility of the difference between the portfolio and the S&P 500 Index returns. For the 50/50 weighted portfolio, the information ratio is 0.7, while that for the 60/40 portfolio it is 0.9. The results are shown in Figure 5.10 on page 187.

Portfolio Rebalancing

The next step is to adjust the portfolio for different bonds and stocks. The cumulative return in Figure 5.10 measures a price return from December 2005 until January 2015. The return assumes the portfolios are "static." That is, the amount invested remains in the same bonds and stocks, and does not change. In reality, stock and bond picking is actively managed. The portfolio at some point would see changes because of new opportunities. The timing of the change

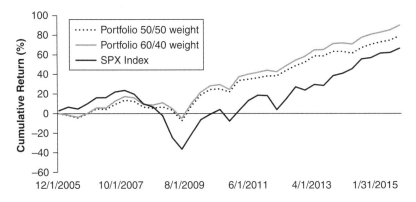

Figure 5.10 Cumulative return of portfolios.

Source: FRB. Cumulative = monthly cumulative price return 12/31/2005–1/31/2015.

in portfolio constituents is important. If an investor takes a "relative value" approach, the timing is ad hoc. Relative value between securities generally happens when sudden market changes or dislocations appear. Relative value can also appear because of larger trends in the market place, in which certain sectors or segments see a significant change in relative performance. In the frameworks discussed previously, the assumption is to use methods of picking bonds and stocks that can be applied when relative opportunities are present. The timing should in general be driven by macroeconomic developments. That is, an investor should look less at the intraday relative value, and instead spot trends that show that a larger relative value has opened up over the previous three months to a year. Relative value is also about comparison. An investor can compare the six bonds and stocks listed to peer companies and look at spreads, multiples, ratios, and yield differences.

Relative Value and Switches

In this example, the first step is to look within the sectors for a trend in relative value. In bonds, the most straightforward approach to switch positions is to look at a historical spread difference. If the maturity of the bonds (the switch candidates) is relatively close but there is a yield/coupon difference, there may be a switch opportunity. This switch opportunity can also be a cross-over relative value like switching the stock for a bond. The relationship between the bond price and the stock price difference is a relevant measure in that regard. If the bonds of a peer company appear to have value, the capital structure analysis may provide give an indication of whether the stock has value. The carry return comparison can also be included by comparing the sum of the bond and stock carry versus other companies. The investor should additionally look at the marketplace newly issued bonds. Corporations issue bonds every day, and a new issue may come at a discount to an existing issue. There is also a beta between bonds and stocks. The stock beta is the tendency of a security's returns to respond to swings in the stock market. The bond beta represents how the bond's returns relate to the returns of the financial market in general. The beta analysis applied to both the bond and stock versus the S&P 500 Index may also provide a measure of return relative value.

The portfolio rebalance maintains the same weights and bond/equity exposure. The changes in some of the credit names will be based on a peer to peer basis, to remain the same weights in a particular sector. The Tips and Treasury bonds are switched to seven-year maturity to add a carry return from the yield curve slope. The macro reason is that, although some tightening by the Fed can expected in the future, the yield curve may stay upward sloping. The two reasons for a positively sloped yield curve are that short-term interest rates stay well below pre-2008 crisis levels and that inflation may gradually rise to 2 percent in the next few years. Together, they should be somewhat reflected in long maturity bonds' term premium as compensation for moderately higher short-term interest rates and inflation. The term premium at the margin should provide investors a carry and roll down return.

In the stocks and bonds shown in Tables 5.4 and in Table 5.5 on page 190, there are some switch ideas to explore. A common practice to identify relative value is to switch bonds and stocks that trade within the same sector. Some companies, however, have a cross-over in terms of activities. Such is the case, for example, with Apple and Amazon. Amazon services customers through low prices, prompt delivery, and an ever-expanding array of services and products that can be ordered online. What sets Amazon apart from competitors is that it has a large free cash flow and access to abundant cash from capital markets. Apple is flushed with cash and had reportedly close to $177 billion of cash as of Q4 2014. Their activities on a stand-alone basis are not the same, but through Amazon, Apple's prime products are sold, and Amazon and both compete in the television business. Another "tweak" to the portfolio is to switch Verizon into AT&T. Verizon may be a longer term play on overall credit improvement as the company had a plan to sell off assets to pay off its long-term debt. AT&T, in contrast, has a large number of network assets as a result of secular demand for wireless communications. Lastly, another switch may be from Amgen into Johnson & Johnson. Amgen has a lower credit quality (BBB+ rated) than Johnson & Johnson (AA-). Amgen has a strong operating profile and diversified product portfolio, whereas Johnson & Johnson has a defensive, noncyclical business and limited leverage. Table 5.5 shows the six companies, compared in terms of credit metrics. From a fundamental and credit point

Table 5.5 Credit comparison

(FY 2015)	AT&T	Verizon	Amazon	Apple	Amgen	Johnson & Johnson
P/E	14	13	101	19	16	18
Price to Book	2	15	14	6	5	4
Price to Free cash flow	12	14	85	11.90	15.90	13.20
Free Cash flow ($, mln)	1,319	16,647	1,770	30,505	7,037	14,295
Liquidity ($, mln)	13,603	13,756	8,883	177,955	29,526	35,495
Net Debt ot EV	3x	2.2x	0.2x	0.1x	1.2x	-0.6x
EBITDA/Interest	11.3x	9.7x	37.9x	137.2x	9.5x	50.6x
Rating	A3/A-	Baa1/BBB+	Baa1/AA-	Aa1/AA+	Baa1/A	A3/A
Beta (bond\stock)	0.95\0.65	0.57\0.75	1.13\0.99	1.07\0.77	0.59\1.01	1.23\0.878
Carry (bps) (bond\stock)	5.9/10.5	8.8\4.4	17\0	18\0	12\0	21\7.5
OAS Spread (bps) (bond)	195	225	205	116	189	115

Source: SEC data, FY 2015.

of view, the switches are more or less "up in quality" in terms of credit rating, free cash flow, and leverage profile (net debt to enterprise value for example).

Choice of Stocks and Bonds

The second decision concerns whether to switch the stock or switch the bonds between these companies. The capital structure model may help answer that, for example, in the case of Apple (as discussed in chapter 3), the low leverage makes its stock "overvalued" relative to what is the optimal capital structure. That means the Apple bonds may be somewhat "undervalued," as compared to Amazon, where the capital structure is somewhat better balanced and the bonds may look to have less value. In a securities picking framework, there has to be an additional "checklist," which consists of criteria to say there is relative value to justify a switch of securities in a portfolio. In summary, the following is a list of criteria an investor should look at when identifying suitable candidates for changing the portfolio:

1) The yield, price, or spread difference gained from the securities switch has to be reasonable to generate a higher excess return.
2) The yield, price, or spread difference should show a historical divergence from a long-term average. In addition, the switch should provide positive carry.
3) The transaction costs of the switch should be relatively low, and the liquidity profile of the portfolio should not be materially affected.
4) The switch should be a credit or liquidity quality improvement that offers appropriate diversification.
5) The change of individual securities should not alter the duration, convexity and volatility risk of the portfolio unless there is a specific purpose to do so.

6) Switching securities has to take into account the correlation with the broader market. That is, the newly selected securities should not have more correlation with the market index than previous securities.

An investor can create charts to compare securities. Another way is to establish a matrix that answers the six points on the checklist shown in Table 5.6 on page 193, in which at the lower end beta, carry, and OAS spread are included in the equity and debt metrics.

In this comparison, the example switch would be AT&T stock for Verizon stock based on lower beta, lower price to book, and modestly better equity valuation. The Verizon bond, however, would remain in the portfolio. For Apple, the stock relative to Amazon may look more appealing on a beta and a PE multiple basis considering the larger difference in OAS spread (partly because of rating) between the respective bonds. Last, Amgen relative to Johnson & Johnson seems fair in terms of stock multiples, but JNJ has significant amount of cash flow that covers the debt (including a much better bond rating). The switch in this case is between Amgen and JNJ bonds. When an investor makes these changes to the portfolio, the portfolio weights are kept the same. Figure 5.11 on page 194 shows the cumulative performance of a 50/50 weighted and a 60/40 weighted portfolio versus the S&P 500 Index. Although the cumulative returns on both portfolios are lower than the portfolios shown previously before the switches were made, the information ratios improved to 0.95. That likely has to do with the improved quality of credit that results in a lower portfolio standard deviation (18 percent compared to 27 percent before the rebalance). The bond and equity duration remains about the same (25 years), but the portfolio carry improves from 17bps/unit of risk to about 25bps/ unit of

Table 5.6 Relative value metrics

(FY 2015)	AT&T	Verizon	Amazon	Apple	Amgen	Johnson & Johnson
P/E	14	13	101	19	16	18
Price to Book	2	15	14	6	5	4
Price to Free cash flow	12	14	85	11.90	15.90	13.20
Free Cash flow ($, mln)	1,319	16,647	1,770	30,505	7,037	14,295
Liquidity ($, mln)	13,603	13,756	8,883	177,955	29,526	35,495
Net Debt ot EV	3x	2.2x	0.2x	0.1x	1.2x	-0.6x
EBITDA/Interest	11.3x	9.7x	37.9x	137.2x	9.5x	50.6x
Rating	A3/A-	Baa1/BBB+	Baa1/AA-	Aa1/AA+	Baa1/A	A3/A
Beta (bond\stock)	0.95\0.65	0.57\0.75	1.13\0.99	1.07\0.77	0.59\1.01	1.23\0.878
Carry (bps) (bond\stock)	5.9\10.5	8.8\4.4	17\0	18\0	12\0	21\7.5
OAS Spread (bps) (bond)	195	225	205	116	189	115
Spread vol.\stock vol. (bps\%)	20\25%	22\27%	19\24%	27\35%	18\22%	19\20%
Transaction cost (bps)	3bps\2cts	4bps\4cts	3bps\2cts	2.5bps\3cts	5bps\4cts	3bps\3cts

Source: SEC, January 2015 valuation for beta/carry and OAS. OAS spread of the 30-year bond of the specific company. Beta is calculated on linear regression with ten-year history. Carry = bond carry/unit of bond duration & equity carry/unit of equity duration. Transaction costs for stocks and bonds are derived from TRACE. Volatility is OAS spread volatility annualized in bps, and stock option realized volatility 3mths annualized.

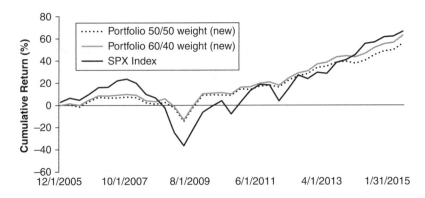

Figure 5.11 Cumulative return of the rebalanced portfolios.

Source: FRB. Cumulative = monthly cumulative price return 12/31/2005–1/31/2015. Amazon stock switched for Apple stock, Verizon stock switched for AT&T, and Amgen bond switched for JNJ.

risk. The total return of both portfolios tracks closer the S&P 500 Index total return. The "up in quality" has made the active portfolio more defensive and it resembles more closely the index. At times of higher volatility, that may be desired.

Conclusion: When and When Not to Pick

Whether an investor is active or passive, stock and bond picking plays a material role in portfolio construction and asset allocation. The slightest tweaks to a portfolio can make a significant difference, as the examples in Figures 5.10 and 5.11 have demonstrated. A passive investor may say that stock/bond picking does not apply to her portfolio. However, a passive portfolio means selecting an index. When a portfolio is invested in an index, it is also invested the constituents of that index. Every year (or in many cases every month), the index rebalances for new securities that replace for older ones that have matured or dropped out of the index because of a downgrade or bankruptcy. A passive investor should therefore be as much concerned with securities selection as an active investor. Most of all, as the previous examples have shown, combining an active and passive strategy may provide maximum diversification and stable return per a lower unit of risk. In today's large universe of securities and funds, there is not a specific fund or strategy that is the "ultimate stock/bond picker." The ability to successfully select securities is tied to a fund manager or a team of professionals who have demonstrated consistent performance. But even then, as discussed in chapter one, an investor must continuously conduct due diligence as things can turn even for the best investors. Investors can be successful pickers themselves if they follow a disciplined approach. In that regard, every fund, strategy, or individual portfolio that an investor chooses is essentially an assembly of securities picks, regardless of whether those strategies or funds are passive or active. The methodologies of bond and stock picking that are discussed in this book can be also be applied to mutual funds, ETFs, or closed-end funds. Investors may choose to combine individual securities and invest a portion in mutual or closed-end funds. The choice of a passive or active approach should then also be determined by expense ratios. On average, passive investment strategies have an expense ratio of only 0.12 percent, while active strategies are around 0.25 percent, according to Morningstar Research. An investor should look at the expense ratio closely as well as the liquidity profile of the funds.

Exchange trade funds (ETFs) are in principle mutual funds, but they have a different structure. ETFs are traded through the day like individual stocks or bonds. Mutual fund, in contrast, can be purchased only once a day. The investor can redeem her mutual fund shares at the Net

Asset Value, which is the market value of the fund that gets struck daily. ETFs made their introduction in the 1990s, and today there 1,300 ETFs with over $ 1.9 trillion in assets, according to Deutsche Bank research. The majority of ETFs are index ETFs, with just a small percentage consisting out actively managed. ETFs are a good example of portfolios that greatly rely on individual picks because the reference portfolio often attempts to mimic an index with an active strategy. In ETFs, an investor can easily combine a stock index with a bond index, unlike in a mutual fund, which is benchmarked to an index. There are no futures contracts on a bond index available, unlike in stocks, where index futures are common. An index future is somewhat comparable to an index ETF as such futures contracts give the investor access to the broader market. Thus ETFs have been created to provide investors access to the broad universe of bond indices, such as the Barclays Aggregate Bond Index. By selecting ETFs on stock and bond indices and weighting them accordingly, an investor can mimic a cross-over portfolio at low transaction cost and high liquidity. An investor can also manage an international strategy by purchasing ETFs where the reference portfolio is invested in foreign stocks or bonds. An advantage is that the investor does not have to be concerned with managing currency risk themselves because foreign ETFs can be settled in domestic currency. It should be noted that in general ETFs do not come without risk, and their volatility can be high.

There is another set of funds, and those are closed-end funds (CEF). A closed-end fund issues a fixed number of shares and reinvests the proceeds in the underlying assets. The shares of closed-end funds are also traded on the stock exchange, but unlike mutual funds, they are not redeemable by stockholders at the NAV. Closed-end funds are known for their share prices trading at significant discounts or premiums to the NAV. A strategy is to buy closed-end funds with the deepest discount to NAV and sell them with the largest premium under the assumption that discounts and premiums mean revert toward the NAV. A CEF is an example of a "cross-over" strategy. A CEF's shares trade like an individual stock on an exchange, while the reference portfolio of the fund can be solely invested in bonds. In the Income, Municipal, US Treasury, and Total Return sectors, there are fixed-income CEFs where shares trade at times at a deep discount to the net asset value. A CEF is concerned with paying regular dividend. The dividend is derived from income sources like coupon interest, option premiums, and carry earned from the yield curve, currency, or credit spread. An investor can select a fixed-income CEF and manage a cross-over strategy by actively trading the shares of the fund while "passively" managing the underlying bond portfolio, earning regular dividend. A caveat is that the liquidity of CEFs is less than that of ETFs, and volatility can be high during certain times of market stress.

A Few Final Words From the Author

To be a consistent stock or bond picker requires discipline for detail and consistency in framework. If the valuation framework frequently changes, the likelihood of success in discovering value may be lower. Although stock/bond picking is not systematic, there are models that use a large number of variables to identify the right picks. The author of this book hopes the reader can use some of frameworks and variables outlined here. Whether investors choose a quantitative or qualitative approach, the choice of an individual security is always a unique choice because that is when the decision is made to pick or not to pick. There will always be stock pickers who just look at stocks, and there will always be bond pickers who only look at bonds. The author of this book hopes the ideas presented may bridge some of the gap between stock and bond pickers. The double digit returns stocks have historically experienced is also possible to achieve in bonds by applying some of the stock-picking methods and maintaining prudent risk management on the higher volatility an investor would have to accept. The stable, more conservative returns that are typical for bonds can be replicated in stocks by using ideas such as carry in the final stock analysis. In the end, stocks and bonds live together in today's fast moving financial market that is highly correlated. There is therefore more need to learn from stock and bond picking to navigate successfully a volatile global marketplace.

Bibliography

Chapter 1

Adrian, Tobias, and Michael Fleming. "The Recent Bond Market Selloff in Historical Perspective" Liberty Street Economics, August 2013. http://libertystreeteconomics.newyorkfed.org/2013/08/the-recent-bond-market-selloff-in-historical-perspective.html#.VOFnmOl0yUk.

Bernanke, Ben. "Deflation: Making Sure 'It' Doesn't Happen Here." Remarks before the National Economists Club, Washington, DC, November 21, 2002. http://www.federalreserve.gov/boarddocs/speeches/2002/20021121/default.htm

Bernanke, Ben. "Long-Term Interest Rates." At the Annual Monetary /Macroeconomics Conference: The Past and Future of Monetary Policy, sponsored by Federal Reserve Bank of San Francisco, San Francisco, California. http://www.federalreserve.gov/newsevents/speech/bernanke20130301a.htm

Bernanke, Ben. "Reflections on the Yield Curve and Monetary Policy." Remarks before the Economic Club of New York, New York, New York, March 20, 2006, http://www.federalreserve.gov/newsevents/speech/bernanke20060320a.htm.

Fabozzi, Frank. *The Handbook of Fixed Income Securities*. New York: McGraw-Hill, 1997.

Gordon, Myron J. "Dividends, Earnings and Stock Prices." *Review of Economics and Statistics* 41, no. 2 (1959): 99–105.

Graham, Benjamin. *Securities Analysis*. New York: McGraw-Hill, 1934.

Greenspan, Alan. *The Federal Reserve's Semiannual Monetary Policy Report*. Before the Committee on Banking, Housing, and Urban Affairs, US Senate, February 26, 1997. http://www.federalreserve.gov/boarddocs/hh/1997/february/testimony.htm.

Kim, Don H., and Jonathan H Wright. "An Arbitrage-Free Three-Factor Term Structure Model and the Recent Behavior of Long-Term Yields and Distant-Horizon Forward Rates." Federal Reserve Board, 2005.

Krugman, Paul. "Dow 36,000: How Silly Is It? " MIT website commentary, 2006. MIT, http://web.mit.edu/krugman/www/dow36K.html.

Laughlin, Laura Silva. "Luck vs. Skill: What Bill Gross and Bill Miller Have in Common," *Fortune Magazine*, March 18, 2014. http://fortune.com/2014/03/18/luck-vs-skill-what-bill-gross-and-bill-miller-have-in-common/.

Modigliani, F., and M. Miller. "The Cost of Capital, Corporation Finance and the Theory of Investment." *American Economic Review* 48, no. 3 (1958): 261–297.

Ross, Stephen, Randolph Westerfield, and Jeffrey Jaffe. *Corporate Finance*. 7th ed. New York: McGraw-Hill, 2005.

Shiller, Robert. *Irrational Exuberance*. Princeton: Princeton University Press, 2000.

Tobin, James. "A General Equilibrium Approach to Monetary Theory," *Journal of Money, Credit, and Banking* 1, no. 1 (1969): 15–29.

Chapter 2

Burghardt, Galen. *The Treasury Bond Basis: An In-Depth Analysis for Hedgers, Speculators and Arbitraguers*. 3rd ed. New York: McGraw-Hill, 2005.

Galitz, Lawrence. *The Handbook of Financial Engineering*. 3rd ed. London: FT Press, 2013.

Illmanen, Antti. *Expected Returns*.London; Wiley, 2011.

Macauley, Frederick. *The Movements of Interest Rates. Bond Yields and Stock Prices in the United States since 1856*. New York: National Bureau of Economic Research, 1938.

Plona, Christopher. *The European Bond Basis: An In-Depth Analysis for Hedgers, Speculators, & Arbitrageurs*. New York: McGraw-Hill, 1996.

Chapter 3

Damodaran, Aswath. *The Dark Side of Valuation*. 2nd ed. New York: FT Press, 2009.

Modigliani, F., and M. Miller. "The Cost of Capital, Corporation Finance and the Theory of Investment." *American Economic Review* 48, no. 3 (1958): 261–297.

Chapter 4

Black, Fisher. "Noise." *Journal of Finance*, 41 (1986): 529–543.

Hull, John. *Options, Futures and Other Derivatives*. 9th ed. New York: Prentice Hall, 2014.

Passareilli, Dan. *Trading Options Greeks: How Time, Volatility, and Other Pricing Factors Drive Profits*. 2nd ed. New York: Bloomberg Press, 2012.

Chapter 5

Graham, Benjamin. *The Intelligent Investor: The Definitive Book on Value Investing*. Rev. ed. New York: HarperBusiness, 2006.

Patro, Dilip, Louis R. Piccotti, and Yangru Wu. "Exploiting Closed-End Fund Discounts: The Market May Be Much More Inefficient Than You Thought." *Social Science Research Network*, July 18, 2014. http://papers.ssrn.com/sol3/papers.cfm?abstract_id=2468061.

Index